'JUST BARK BACK - HE'LL UNDERSTAND YOU'

By

Ann Douglas

Some 'words of wisdom' about how to go about living
with a dog without tearing your hair out

Published by Dolman Scott Ltd

Copyright Ann Douglas

Illustrations by Katy Dynes

ISBN 978-1-905553-41-9

Dolman Scott
www.dolmanscott.com

Foreword

I spent the first twenty years of my working life with horses, and I quickly came to the conclusion that they were big and it hurt when they didn't behave themselves, so training them was essential if my health was to survive.

Eventually I was able to have a dog of my own and it seemed pretty important that it was trained well enough so that I could enjoy it, eventually I went from being a member of the training class to being the instructor, and over ten years later people who came to me originally with puppies are coming back with their next puppies.

From necessity I only see people when they turn up at class, so there is a lot of time when they are on their own with their dogs, and this book started when people asked me questions and talked about problems they had.

I am not a training enthusiast – I don't train for the sake of it, I just aim for having a dog that is very easy to live with the minimum of effort going in and the maximum of pleasure coming out.

The following is written by a very stressed out woman who came to me in desperation – she is not so stressed these days!

Chester

I had my heart set on getting a black Labrador, eventually the timing was right and so one day in March 2008 I set off to look at a litter of black puppies. All adorable, I was faced with the hard decision of which one to choose, when out the corner of my eye I spotted this dark yellow puppy chewing on a stick. It wasn't the black bitch that I had gone to get but he looked so cute and with his ridge on his nose it was love at first sight.

I guess looking back now, him chewing on the stick should have pre-warned me of what was to follow but alas it didn't and from the second I took him home he was chewing! At first it wasn't too much of an issue as he was only small, it was only a few kids' toys that got consumed but as he got bigger the damage started getting more severe, holes in walls, beds destroyed, in fact anything he could chew Chester chewed!

A year on and I was at breaking point ... thankfully this is when I came across Ann, an absolute godsend! I am so grateful to her and her classes. In a short space of time I had a dog that no longer chewed my house to bits! I could also enjoy walking him without holding on for dear life! Her classes taught me how to discipline Chester and set him boundaries, to teach him who is the boss, and make him understand what he can and can't get away with.

I owe Ann a lot and would like to take this opportunity to say a massive thank you! My only regret is that I didn't find you earlier on as it would have saved a lot of stress and upset for both me and Chester!

So to anyone who is reading this I highly recommend Ann and urge you if you are considering training to begin it as soon as possible, older dogs can of course still be trained but it will be a lot easier for both of you if you begin when they are younger.

Nikki Cross

The most important thing that your dog can
ever learn is that

'His life gets better if he does things
that please you'

The second most important thing that your dog can ever learn is that

If he pleases you then his life will get better

INDEX

1. THE GOOD OLD DAYS

I don't know if I'm being serious about the old days being good - after all the average length of a dog's life was shorter in those days, pet food was whatever was cheapest, and veterinary science was in its infancy, but there were things to recommend it. I think there were more dogs around – after all you had to have a dog to keep the vermin down, more people lived in the countryside and you had to have a dog if you were interested in going poaching for the pot and besides there was more countryside in those days. There was more likely to be someone at home in those days, mothers stayed at home because it was a full time job looking after the family, for necessity fathers spent time digging in the garden, kids went out to play, people walked more – they had to they couldn't afford a car, dogs were definitely not allowed on the furniture, after all humans had spent a long time saving up for it, holidays were a day at the seaside if they were lucky so putting the dog in kennels wasn't a problem.

Dogs weren't spoilt, no one had the money to waste on spoiling pets, people were just lucky if they could afford to feed a dog. Dogs probably understood their places better; they were at the bottom of the pecking order because that's how far the money extended. Money wasn't wasted on therapy, if the dog was a problem it probably got turfed out of the home or drowned in the nearest canal.

But time has moved on and we're mostly more affluent. We have money to spend indulging a dog, although we might not have the time to walk it as much as it needs, but never mind. We'll buy it the best organic doggy dins we can get, and if it gets fat we'll spend money taking it to the vets, using the car of course, and we'll put it in the car to take it to the park to walk it once a day, mostly, and if work or social life gets in the way and means we have to leave it all day then we may employ someone else to walk it!

We have to live in the time we're in, but just don't get carried away with progress and affluence. I'm not saying that if you have to go out to work all day then you shouldn't have a dog, but if you do have a dog you have to give it realistic boundaries and a realistic amount of time, and if you're not prepared to do that then maybe you shouldn't have a dog.

Even if you are quite happy and prepared to replace things that the dog chews up, then just consider what this tells the dog – 'you are so important you can chew whatever you like'. You might be prepared to live with a dog that spends all day in the garden barking at the slightest possible noise or movement, the message the dog gets is 'you are so important you do whatever you like - never mind the neighbours'. Eventually the message that you give the dog is that it is number one in the pack. But number one also has a lot of responsibilities - number one has to be pack leader and protect the pack and this is incredibly stressful for any dog – how does he know that the postman isn't a threat? If a pack member goes out and leaves the pack then how can number one dog protect it? Number one dog doesn't understand humans have to go to work all day so is in a high state of stress not knowing where one of its pack is. Is it any wonder number one dog tries to stop people going out the door? If you go for a walk then number one dog has to chase away other dogs that might be a threat – it can't just enjoy the walk - the responsibilities are too great.

What I am trying to say is that everything you do or say has a message to a dog, if you make sure that the message is what you want it to be then you can make the relationship work so that things go your way, if you go on giving the wrong messages then you may be leading things towards, perhaps not disaster, but to a lot less happy relationship than you were hoping for.

2. WHY BOTHER

Be honest, you're probably wondering 'why bother with this training lark, can't I just own the dog? – that's a lot less effort'. Well no, it isn't, you cannot avoid training a dog that lives with you, it will either learn bad behaviour or good behaviour - but put in a bit of effort initially to understand what you are saying to the dog, and a bit of effort to take him places and teach him a few things, then you will reap the reward throughout your dog's life. People who know you will think 'gosh wasn't she lucky to take on such an easy nice obliging animal' and you will have to grit your teeth silently because you will know how easy it is too screw up a relationship with a dog and you will probably know that it wasn't just down to luck.

It is important that your dog meets other 'nice' dogs, and it is sensible that you at least teach him the basics, so I think that attending a training club is a great idea, but it's not essential, you can do without if you are prepared to think about things and do the work on your own. But if you are thinking of going to a class, go along W I T H O U T Y O U R

D O G and watch a class, and if the thought of going fills you with dread then do not join, go and find a better class; if what they say does not make sense; if the dogs aren't happy; if the class members are bored stiff, then go and find somewhere else. How long you attend is up to you, I guess until you get bored, get satisfied with how your dog behaves, find something else you have to do on that particular evening, decide there's something on the telly you'd rather watch instead, it's up to you, it's your dog, you can take as little out of it as you like.

I initially attended a training class because I'm lazy, I knew it would be less effort owning a well behaved dog than one who was the local hooligan, and I still think that holds good today. Today I run the dog training, what I really want to do is to meet you in five years time and to ask you 'Are you still glad you own your dog?' I want to ask your dog, 'Are you glad you live in the pack that you do?' And I want to ask your neighbour 'Are you happy that them next door own that dog?' If I hear a ' yes' as answer to all three questions then, as the quotation goes, 'my work is done'.

3. HOW IMPORTANT ARE YOU TO YOUR DOG?

Now I'm sure you're very important when it comes to opening the tin of doggy chunks at meal times, but if your dog doesn't take much notice of you at other times then you have a problem. If you've just got a cute little puppy then it will probably very soon learn his name, and if you've just got a rescue dog and it's just received a new name then it will have no idea what it's called. If you've re-homed a working dog from a working home, and we're probably talking mediocre greyhounds here, then just remember that it may never have learned that it has a name at all, some of the moderate dogs from moderate kennels may not have had a relationship with anyone that called it by any name in a nice way.

Names are important, very important, and I'm sure that you decided on his name long ago. But there are some things you've got to think about. The first thing to remember is that if the dog has got a long name then he will react principally to the first part of the name. If he's called Samuel then it doesn't really matter if you shout 'Sam', 'Samuel' 'Samson' or 'Sammy' he's going to react to the first part of the name. Just consider whether the name sounds like an instruction, if you call your dog, for example 'Noel', your dog will hear the first part only, and will probably get very confused when you spend your life yelling 'No' at him, alternatively if he ignores the instruction 'no' then he'll wonder why you get mad.

If you've got a family there's another thing that might confuse him, if you've named your dog 'Flopsie Fifi Trixiebell' then don't be too surprised if your macho rugby playing partner chooses to call it Tyson when they're out on their own, and perhaps sixteen year old daughter chooses to call it Beckham, and twenty year old son chooses to call it by whatever trendy name he likes at the moment – the poor dog probably doesn't know whether he's coming or going, he may just cope by ignoring everyone.

If your dog does not respond when you call his name then it's something you have to teach him. Wait until his attention is elsewhere and call his name, with a bit of luck he'll turn round and look at you because you made a sound, then throw him a titbit, repeat when his attention is elsewhere, if he's not stupid then he'll work out that it's worth while looking at you when you make a particular sound (his name). If he doesn't look at you then do something strange to get his attention, jump up and down, take your clothes off, anything but keep repeating his name. If he totally seems to ignore any sounds then whip him off to the vets to find out if he is actually deaf, it does happen and it's easier to find out now.

Second problem is overload, this is a dog you've got, not Einstein. By all means use his name to get his attention, but then shut up, you do not have to repeat the name every ten seconds, the dog knows that it's him you are talking to. If you use his name when you don't need to, then he will stop listening to it. When you do use his name then try and give it pleasant associations, you want your dog to think 'Oh Mum mentioned my name, I had better go and see what she wants' but if you call 'Fido come here and get a telling off' then it's not really surprising if he doesn't come is it? I'm not suggesting that he doesn't get the telling off if he needs it, but don't associate bad things with his name, **his name is special.**

Equally important is the phrase 'good boy/girl'. When your dog hears this then it tells the dog that he is doing something right, that you approve of what he is doing. If you use this phrase when the dog is doing something that is wrong then you've just told the dog that what he is doing is right, so why should things improve? A lot of people throw in the phrase when they ask the dog to do something in the hope that this will make the dog behave, this doesn't make sense, it doesn't work like that, and this is a dog you are talking to not a psychologist!

Sometimes you want your dog to come to you - then by all means use his name, but if you want your dog to stay where he is then don't use his name. Names mean nice warm cuddly experiences, but your dog has to have a certain amount of courage to stay away from you so don't tempt him to come to you by using his name.

When he gets the idea that it's worth his while paying attention to you then attempt to get his attention when he doesn't want to give it, for example, if he's just met another dog on a walk then the other dog is infinitely more interesting than you are, initially don't try and call your dog because there is no way he's going to listen to you, but when he's said hello, then maybe, when you say his name he'll look at you. Eventually you'll find that you can interrupt when the stakes are higher and he's, for example, playing with an exciting puppy, or when it matters, when he's thinking of going off chasing a flock of sheep.

Can you see how it's got more important, this isn't a party trick, this is something that could save his life and what is possibly more important, it can make your life a lot easier on a day to day basis? It could matter to a point of life and death that your dog will listen to an instruction, 'Come here off that railway line because there's a train coming'; 'don't go and chase that horse', 'don't go and annoy that aggressive looking dog that's licking its lips'.

You might think that it only matters that your dog obeys orders, but dogs soon learn to tune out instructions and suffer from 'selective deafness' if it is allowed to get away with it. Your dog will not obey an order that it does not hear.

When you are out and about you will hear people shouting at their dogs, the dog may be only five feet away, but it is so used to only listening when an order is shouted that it thinks that spoken orders are not for him. Don't get into a habit of shouting unless 1) your dog is a distance away or 2) your dog is deaf. That is the only acceptable reason, why shout? It's hard work, teach your dog to listen to a spoken command. Alternatively if it ever does end up in a situation when it really does matter then you can shout for all you are worth and your dog will know that he'd better do what you are shouting straight away because this is important.

4. IN THE BEGINNING

I'm assuming you're reading this because you've either just got a dog or you've got so fed up with your dog that you've realised that you've got to do something. This being so, I'm not going to go on about what sort of dog to buy that's going to perfectly fit in with your lifestyle. You've got what you've got and you've got to do your best with that. What I will say is that you should work out what task your dog was originally bred for. I'm not saying that there aren't dogs which will totally go against the original plan, but it will at least give you a clue.

Dogs that were originally bred to be guard dogs have a tendency to be protective, dogs that were originally bred to be sheepdogs have a tendency to nip at the heels of screaming children, they're not trying to be aggressive, they are trying to round up the children, and this is what they are genetically programmed to do. Dalmatians are bred to run behind the carriages of posh people, they're able to go ten or twenty miles quite easily – any wonder that they aren't content with a walk round the streets once a day? I met someone once with a bulldog, she said she was quite bemused when she had it first as it used to rush out into a field of cows and lie down in the middle of the herd, it's behaviour didn't get any worse than that, but originally part of a bulldogs training was that it needed to lie down in front of a bull so that when the bull came up to sniff it the bulldog could grab the bull's nose!

Remember that if your dog was originally bred as something like a gun dog then it is just possible that it might come from a line of show dogs; the original purpose has been overtaken by showing. Dogs have to be quite bright to work as a gun dog, gamekeepers and their like do not mess about with the sort of dog that doesn't have the brains for it, on the other hand, show dogs do not have to be that intelligent they only have to look pretty.

5. KIND AND POSITIVE TRAINING METHODS

'Kind and positive training methods' are hopefully what I use, and most of the time it works. But I will not lie about it, if my dog _deliberately_ and _knowingly_ disobeys me, at a time when he was perfectly able to comply with my instructions, then I will use punishment! Punishment has to fit the crime, I am not advocating beating up a puppy for piddling on the carpet – because that was your fault for not letting puppy out into the garden soon enough.

Punishment can be as mild as frowning at a dog - with some dogs that is all they need. Punishment can consist of putting a treat back in your pocket or by not praising your dog when it complies – perhaps it was a rubbish sit anyway, but, just suppose, your dog runs off to chase a rabbit when he was told not to, then, when he eventually comes back, making him walk to heel for the next five minutes. If he does it a second time then perhaps making him walk to heel for ten minutes. An alternative punishment is giving your dog a good thrashing – but then your dog might think 'well hang on – if I'm going to get thrashed for going back then I may as well not go back until I'm good and ready'.

What you have got to remember is that it is the tone of your voice and your manner that tells the dog how cross you are. It's not going to worry the dog at all if you give him a

10

thorough telling off in a laughing happy voice, the dog doesn't understand the words you are using (not even my dogs are this clever!) but he will recognise the tone of your voice. My ultimate sanction is telling the dog 'if you do that again then I will pull your legs off', and you have to sound like you mean it!

If your dog does something really terrible and you are tempted into actually beating him, then just stop, put the dog away, go and have a cup of tea or something stronger. Beating him will not ultimately work because your dog will survive it, and if he has survived it once then you have nothing worse to threaten him with. What you want your dog to think is 'gosh that thing I did got him really mad, I had better not do that again or he really will pull my legs off.'

If your dog does something really terrible and all I can think of here is some vicious act, then you have to seriously think about either taking professional advice (and I am talking <u>serious</u> professional advice here, from someone who you will have to pay considerable amounts to and get advice that works), or putting the dog to sleep. It might be drastic action but it has to be considered. Never re-home a vicious animal with the possible exception of the police or one of the services - it would still be your fault if he attacked anyone.

6. LEAD WALKING

This is not teaching you dog to walk 'Crufts' style to heel, this is to establish a way of walking that is comfortable and enjoyable for you both. Ideally this should all start when your dog is a cute little puppy. The trouble is, it's no effort for you to cope with a cute little puppy that is pulling on the lead, but your cute little puppy may grow up to be something that is a cross between a pit bull terrier and a cart horse, and pulling on the lead is not so funny then. Also consider everyone else who walks the dog - if you've got a big strong husband (or wife - why should I be sexist!) then just be aware if they are letting the puppy pull. And consider, you might be fit and healthy now, but bad backs happen and can stop you walking your dog if it doesn't know how to walk nicely. And if you've got kids that are growing at a nice rate, then maybe they'll be happy to walk to the dog when they are old enough, but if the dog pulls like an express train they won't be so keen. Furthermore, consider you might be able to cope with the pulling now, but with luck you'll own this dog for ten or fifteen years, will you still be happy to be pulled along when you are ten years older than you are now? Another thought, you may hope that a 'friend' might look after Puppy when you go on holiday, it'll save a fortune in kennel fees, but I can guarantee that if you let Puppy grow into a hooligan everyone will suddenly decide there is a reason they can't possibly have it to stay.

- FACT - The lead is not like a tow rope that has to be tight for it to be working.
- FACT - A dog has to have someone on the other end of the lead to pull against for him to be able to pull at all! This means that if your dog pulls it is because you let him.
- FACT - A lead is something that is necessary for you to control the dog in <u>unusual</u> circumstances when your restraint is needed.

It is perfectly possible to teach your dog to walk to heel because he knows this is what you want him to do, but it is more effective if you convince your dog that he wants to walk at heel because this is the place he wants to be.

Most dogs pull because they believe that it will get them to where they want to go quicker than walking to heel – how many dogs pull when they know they are going to the vets? Consider when your dog pulls in front of you simply stopping, not saying anything - not speaking, your dog will wonder what you are doing and will sooner or later stop pulling at the lead and come back to your leg, at this point you can suddenly walk on again – so your dog is then rewarded for being in the right position by you walking on again, <u>by you effectively doing exactly what the dog wanted you to do</u>.

Now it might seem odd that at this stage you are not talking to the dog, not telling him off for pulling on the lead telling him where to be, we actually want the dog to work things out for himself, if he can work out what to do and what not to do then he will work out that it is pretty silly trying to pull because that makes you stop walking. This makes the dog responsible for his actions, he wants to get to the park faster, but every time he starts to pull he causes you to not go faster but instead to stop. Once the dog has worked out for himself what is happening it is a short step to not pulling at all – pulling is not productive.

It is very tempting when you are lead walking if the dog pulls on ahead to correct him and bring him back to the right position – and possibly to reward him once he is in the right position, but consider, if you do this too many times (more than three or four) then your dog is not learning too walk in the right position but is actually learning to pull ahead, because he then gets told to get back and he then gets a reward. You <u>MUST NOT</u> reward anything that is caused by bad behaviour! Even if the dog does good behaviour in the end, it will mean that the bad behaviour will be rewarded as well; the only reward for bad behaviour followed by good behaviour is that the dog does not get punished.

But accept that there will be times when a puppy pulls, if there is a dog just in front, if a cat is sitting there – you just have to accept this and ignore it, a puppy cannot learn to control his exuberance when something really exciting happens.

Have a thought for class lessons, it will cause chaos if everyone is stopping and starting, we won't get anywhere, it will resemble a scene on the dodgems, so in those circumstances we don't ask you to suddenly stop, on the other hand the dogs soon learn that they aren't actually going anywhere and choose not to pull anyway.

Once the dog has learnt all this, then there will be times he forgets, usually accidentally on purpose. If he does forge on ahead then it is permissible to remind him with an 'oy' this should be enough for him to remember to get back to the 'ideal' position, if it doesn't work then go back to stopping without speaking, he will soon 'remember' things. Don't fall into the trap of telling him where he should actually be, he knows this, if he hasn't got the sense to know this then he can stand with you until he remembers. If you are not consistent and forget and allow him to pull then he will just fall into the habit of pulling again, and it will take more effort on your part to retrain him again – it's easier not to let him pull!

I haven't mentioned treats yet. The reward for the dog comes when he returns to the right position and gets to walk on again. If you want to further reward the dog there is nothing to stop you giving him a titbit <u>when</u> he is walking nicely in the right position and not pulling, but don't give him a reward for changing from doing something wrong to do something right because that way to get another titbit he has to again do something wrong.

This is all about your dog learning to control himself to your advantage; there is no reason why you should be the only one putting effort into your relationship, if you make it to his benefit to act in a way that works for both of you. Dogs are devious manipulative horrible animals (well apart from mine obviously) that soon learn what works to the dog's benefit – you have to ensure that what works for the dog's benefit is the same thing that benefits you, thinking about things, dogs are a lot like children!

In a class it is easier for the trainer if all the dogs are walking on the same side, traditionally the left; I think it's got something to do with you being able to use your right hand to reach for your sword! But I actually like my dogs to walk so that I am between them and the traffic, so I frequently expect them to walk on my right depending on the side of the road that I'm on. They soon learn to change sides when told, <u>BUT</u> you don't ever want your dog to move in front of you because if he does then one day you will end up falling over him, so they have to go behind me to change sides. Incidentally 'heel' means on the left, 'side' means on the right and they soon get to understand and change sides happily and frequently before they are asked.

This might all seem very basic, but it is worth getting on top of. If you can't control your dog when it is on a lead and a foot away from you then you haven't got much hope when you go on to do something more interesting. Attaching your dog to a lead is very reassuring, but don't ever imagine that a lead is something to force your dog to do what you want him to do; you should be able to cope with a lead that is very thin and fragile. You should be able to hold the lead on one finger because the dog isn't pulling, and your arm should be relaxed and hanging vertically.

There is a vast commercial enterprise making things for dogs, including extending leads, consider, the dog is on a short lead at your side and you decide he can go on ahead, so you let the dog pull because that way the lead gets longer. Effectively, your dog is being rewarded for pulling. I suggest that rewarding your dog for pulling guarantees that he is going to pull again, I'm not saying don't use an extending lead, but be aware of what you are doing and what your are teaching your dog.

Now you've got your dog walking by your side is he concentrating on you or the dog in front, or sniffing the ground, or cocking his leg on every tuft of grass, and does it matter? Well it probably doesn't if you are just going for a walk, but if you are in a class lesson then it certainly does matter. You want your dog to concentrate on you, to listen to you, to stay in position by your leg, if you carry on attending training classes then you'll go on to work without a lead and if the dog isn't concentrating then it isn't going to be able to stay in position because it won't know what you are doing. So in a class don't accept bad behaviour from your dog, it should walk nicely by your leg listening to you. If it tries to sniff the ground than you must get his attention back on you, either verbally, you can actually have a titbit tucked between your fingers (but don't give it as a reward for lifting his head and concentrating on you), you can physically touch him (or push him, or lightly smack him) you can change direction – particularly effective if you walk into him accidentally on purpose, you've got to make the dog think 'I'd really like to sniff the ground but Mother's such a problem I had better concentrate on her because she needs me'.

You and your dog have a relationship where one of you is boss and one of you is the follower, if you do not choose to be the boss then your dog will be the boss, this is how Dogs think and if you don't like it then you shouldn't have got a dog at all. Remember, classes only last for a set time, even if we did lead walking the whole time your dog could cope with doing what you want for an hour, by accepting bad behaviour you let the dog think that he can actually choose what to do, if he thinks this then why should he obey you when it really matters?

Also consider where the dog walks when it is out with you, if it is nicely by your side and with you taking the choice over where you go and at what speed then everything is probably okay. But if the dog is way out in front and he is leading the way then you are allowing him to take control of the walk, you are allowing him to be 'pack leader', is it any wonder that he doesn't obey you when he's let off the lead?

If you're going to continue with training classes then there will be times when you put the dog in a stay and walk away. You should always use the leg nearest to the dog to start a walk when the dog is coming with you, but when the dog is staying put you use the leg furthest away from the dog to start the walk, then the dog is getting another indication of what you are doing and what you want him to do, it's an easy way of giving the dog another silent instruction.

7. THOUGHT FOR THE DAY.

If your dog is walking along nicely by your side, alert and listening to you, then don't just ignore him - remember to praise him occasionally, because if you don't praise him he will do something naughty because that way he will at the very least get your attention.

8. THE PAST

The past is the past, whether your dog had a horrible home before he came to you, or whether you've spent the last six months spoiling him and are now suffering the consequences. Dogs do not dwell in the past, they will not know that you are being exceptionally soft because he had a horrible start to life he will just think you are a pushover and as a consequence he (the dog) will have to be leader of the pack.

Treat your dog the best way you know how - live for today!

9. FIRST CATCH YOUR DOG!

The inherent thing about letting your dog go loose is that he won't come back if he doesn't want to, and unless you are an Olympic athlete you haven't got a hope in hell in running fast enough to catch him, luckily there are several strategies you can use to make him want to come back.

20

Incidentally, if you do run after him he will very soon decide it's a good game, you will ultimately lose weight and you will look very silly in the process - but you won't catch your dog.

The most basic mistake you can make is to take him to the park, let him run and play, and then expect him to come back, have his lead put on and then take him home, he will very soon work out that not coming back means his playtime is extended. What you must do is call him to you, give him a treat, and then tell him to 'go and play'. If coming to you means that mostly something nice happens he will be quite happy to come back to you!

But be careful, he will work out the difference between coming and eating a treat, and having his lead put on and going home, you must call him to you and tell him to sit and take hold of his collar **FIRST** and then give him the treat, then you can choose to either let him go or to end the playtime. You will look very silly indeed if he's just eaten your last treat and then he runs off!

It makes the whole process easier, of course, if he wears a collar all the time, you then have something to take hold of. If he has the sort of coat which means it's difficult to take hold of his collar consider leaving a short length of rope hanging from his collar ready for you to take hold of. If he's the sort of dog that doesn't want you take hold of his collar then think about having him trail a line all the time, hopefully this will let you put your foot on the line and stop him running off. The plastic covered washing line that you can buy is very suitable; it's also cheap enough that if you've got him trailing 20' (feet) of line behind him but you are confident that 15' would be long enough you can chop the end off. This way you never have to make the decision to let him loose without the line, just eventually you will realise it's so short you don't need it any longer. Hopefully your dog will think you are so clever that you can get hold of him so easily it's not worth running off

Calling the dog is necessary, but sometimes you just know he isn't going to come, he really does need to go and say hello to the new dog that's just come in the park, you've got two choices, you can yell at your dog, but he will ignore you - so all you are really teaching him is to ignore you when he chooses. Or you can wait until he's said hello and he's ready to come when he's called, yes, it is a compromise, but this way he doesn't learn to ignore you and he will come when he's called, and you can tell him what a good boy he is and give him a treat for being good. As your dog gets older/better trained then you can call him when he doesn't want to come, and hopefully because it's so ingrained he will come anyway.

If your dog has already worked out that it's better to run away than let himself be caught, then think about telling him to sit, if he's sitting then he can't run away, and you can tell him he's good and give him a titbit, rather than get mad with him. You might have to spend some time training the 'instant' sit in the garden before you try this one for real!

A good way to think about commands is to always be willing to bet £5 that he will obey, if you just know you're going to lose the £5 then don't bother issuing the command. (Send it to me instead!)

I've talked about treats, a treat doesn't always mean food, it can mean food but it can mean a play with a toy, a rub on the tummy, a romp with a handler, a treat is anything that the dog thinks is worth having. Humans go to work for money, if they didn't get wages they wouldn't go, there has to be something in it for them, and there has to be something in it for the dog. Treats don't work if the dog won't look at you, your dog has to realise that it's worth checking with you often, start off around the house by just rewarding eye contact, if he looks throw him a treat (we're talking very small tasty treats here, not a Bonio every time), when he's not next to you then call him and give him a treat when he comes, this is easy for him and very rewarding, but if it doesn't work in the house and garden then there is no way it will work in the park.

Young dogs will stay with you beautifully at first, you're safety, and they won't stray too far. But as they get older they get independent and adventurous and they want to venture forth - they're a bit like stroppy teenage children. You've got to ask yourself, why should they want to stay with you when there are more exciting things happening other places? Just remember when they run off they are probably being rewarded, not by you but by getting to chase a rabbit, put up a pheasant, and bark at a cow, so you've got to make the dog want to keep an eye on you because you are where interesting things happen. You may be thinking here, well I had my old dog for fifteen years and he just plodded along behind me, maybe he did, but you've got a young dog now, the equivalent of a formula one racing car, they have to be taught to want to stay with you. If you have treats in your pocket they can smell them and there is just the chance they'll get one if they are close enough, if your dog is into toys (you do play with him don't you?) then have something in your pocket. You don't necessarily have to throw it all the time, take it out and play with it yourself, just carry it in your hand, make him think 'well I had better stay with her because she's got my ball and she might just throw it'.

If your dog does go too far then there is the dilemma of what you say when he comes back, you can't beat it half to death because that way you just ensure that the recall will get worse. What you can do, as long as the dog is old enough to know that going too far is naughty, is have a treat ready to give it, but DON'T GIVE THE TREAT, tell him that's what he would have had if he had been quicker and put it back in your pocket. A second punishment is to keep the dog with you for a time, you can put him on the lead of course, but if he knows how to walk at heel without the lead then just do this, it makes it much more of a punishment than being on a lead because without a lead the dog has to control himself. At the end of the punishment you can give the dog permission to go play, you are God; you have the power to do this!

Lastly consider, there is the time when your dog isn't going to come back to, but a person is watching and expecting you to call him, there's nothing to stop you calling your dog by a different name! If you call 'Fido, Fido' the watcher will be happy, you will be happy you are appeasing him, the dog will ignore you of course – Fido is not his real name, but then he would of ignored you if you used his real name. But what you haven't done is taught the dog to ignore his real name!

The use of the dog's name should be something the dog welcomes; it should mean to the dog that something good is going to happen. If you call your dog just remember to put some fun in your voice, if you sound suicidal and depressed then the dogs isn't going to want to come – make life fun!

<u>You may think your dog is the worst on earth and ignores you deliberately, just consider he may actually be medically deaf - if you are at all unsure get him checked by the vet</u>

It's tempting to throw sticks, just remember that a number of dogs have ended up at the vets when a stick has bounced badly and the sharp end has ended up stuck in their throats.

If you have more than one dog then there is nothing to stop you only rewarding the first one home! It gives the slower dog a big incentive to come faster next time.

If your dog is down one end of the field and the wind is blowing strongly then he may not be able to hear you call, it's a good idea to teach your dog to come to a visual signal, I put my hands out wide, the dog can see this easily when it's six foot away from you, but when the dog is the other end of the field it's not recognisable!

A true story - I was up the woods with my dogs when I met a chap with a young springer spaniel cross, the chap was trying to bring the dog up properly and he called the dog back to him and rewarded it when it came and sent the dog off again. But he did have a problem, he knew at the end of the walk the dog wouldn't come back. I was a bit surprised and sure enough what he said was true, but what he didn't say was that when he wanted to finish the walk he got the lead out of him pocket and it was only when the dog saw the lead that the dog suddenly decided not to come. I think the dog was smarter than his owner.

10. BRAMBLE

It will come with great amusement to everyone who ever knew Bramble that she has appeared in a book on dog training; Bramble was to dog training what I am to super models. I knew Bramble a long time ago when she was owned by a friend of mine, he was a typical small scale farmer who had a lot of assets to his name, but never any money. His pleasure in the winter was pheasant shooting, and he had Bramble to assist him. Bramble did not believe that she needed his help or his instructions or his training. Bramble was a very good 'larder filler' but she did not fit the image of being a loyal trustworthy well behaved companion to a shooting gent. There was a river crossing the land and when it was in full flood in the winter it was quite formidable. On occasions pheasants used to land on the wrong side of it, when the river was swollen with winter rain it was judged to be too fast for the dogs to attempt, and then Bramble would decide for herself that someone ought to go across and get the bird and over she would go despite her Dad telling her not to, and she would struggle up the other side, spend ages searching, pick up the bird, battle again with the swollen river, climb up the bank and then, when the going was at last easy and everyone was watching and being very impressed, and her Dad was visibly swelling with pride, she would drop the bird and then walk away - no longer interested!

I lived with the family, and eventually it was decided to let Bramble have pups, and I was very quick to offer to have one of the pups so that the family would have the pleasure of knowing the pup but not have the bother of keeping one themselves. The deed was done, I was in a state of high excitement because this was to be my first dog, and quite reasonably Bramble got a bit fatter towards the end. Come the due date nothing happened, and after a week we concluded that Bramble had decided for herself not to be a mum. They kindly let me go out and buy a pup for myself. I bought Tacit home and it was now well over ten weeks since Bramble was last mated and that night she decided to produce the one very large pup that she was carrying! Bramble had done her own thing again. The pup of course stayed with the family, and although her Dad loved her dearly and you could never describe her as a beauty, she went on to be a good dog - but never as good as her Mum.

Meanwhile I got in the habit of coming home from work, having a cup of tea, and then taking Tacit out for a walk. Bramble got in the habit of coming with us. I was in a dilemma in one way, because I knew very well that she would not come when she was called, but as I was mostly walking on her owner's land it didn't matter that much, and as I liked having her along I let her come, but I knew my limitations - I only ever called her when she was coming anyway. This worked well for a lot of time, then I made the mistake of calling her early, and she came! It had become a habit by then, although it was probably helped by the fact that she was now well into middle age, and she actually grew into quite an agreeable companion. Her end was sad, she chose to avoid walking under an electric fence that was switched off and was so high it wouldn't have touched her anyway, and went onto a road in the dark where she was struck by a lorry. We had four other dogs living at the house at the time but the pack was considerably smaller without her.

I'm telling you this because I want you to realise that there is usually more than one way of doing things, I also want you to accept that you can 'always teach on old dog new tricks' and lastly I want you to accept that although dogs are stupid in that none of them have ever passed an exam at college, sometimes, and at some things, they are incredibly clever and talented.

11. CRIME AND PUNISHMENT

Now, I'm not suggesting that you're going to get into punishment in a serious way, but there's probably going to be times when your dog's halo is going to slip, and you'll have a difference of opinion or two, but keep in mind you've got the ultimate control - you're the only one who can open a tin of doggo chunks in meaty jelly.

The days of Barbara Woodhouse and heavy discipline is over, mainly because we've discovered there were better ways to train animals, it's better if we give the animal the option of doing it 'right' because it's more beneficial to the dog that way - life is also a lot more fun for you if you make it your life's work to have a dog that enjoys pleasing you!

The first and most important thing you've got to remember is PRAISE YOUR DOG IF IT'S DOING IT RIGHT. The worse thing to most dogs is to be ignored, so if that's the reaction they get when they're doing something right then they will probably change to doing something wrong just so they get some attention.

Now we should talk about praise, praise cannot be interpreted by you, it has to be what your dog thinks is praise - so you might be giving out the titbits; or playing with the dog; or rubbing it's tummy; or throwing a ball; or playing with a tuggy; or letting it off the lead or even just smiling at it; or talking in a daft happy voice. Some people refuse to praise the dog, they use the argument that 'the dog should do what I ask because I'm the master' - oh get real. How often would you go to work if you didn't get wages? Yes, you've got an argument, but it's an argument that doesn't stand up if you want to have a happy willing pet which does things to please you. I am not condemning you to a lifetime of giving your dog a titbit every time you ask it to sit down, this is for TRAINING, for when your dog doesn't have a clue what the word sit means. At the first stage why not give your dog treats for trying, once your dog understands what the word sit means then you can ration your rewards to the best sits, or the fastest sit, or the straightest neatest quickest sit.

What you shouldn't let your dog believe is that, however well he does something, he will never ever get praise or reward, because the cold hard facts are that he will give up trying. On the other hand he mustn't think that however badly he does something it doesn't matter because he will get a reward anyway. Even when your dog is ninety and staggering round with a Zimmer frame, just occasionally it is worth giving praise or a titbit for something like a sit or a come.

It is a scientific fact that rewards work better on a variable schedule, in English this means the dog gets rewarded sometimes, so the dog lives in hope and keeps trying.

Punishment often means 'lack of reward', it wasn't good enough to get a reward - better try harder next time. Usually that's sufficient, but sometimes the dog rewards itself, for example instead of performing the exercise at club it goes and sniffs all of the other dogs, then you catch it again. Now you don't give it a titbit, but on the other hand, it's had a jolly good time sniffing the other dogs, what you've got to get the dog to understand is that you are sufficiently angry so that if he does it again you'll 'rip its legs off' okay I'm exaggerating here, but do you understand what I'm saying - you have to make the dog think that 'okay it was great going to the other dogs, but mum/dad was so angry it really wasn't worth it'. If you can do this life will get better, if you can't you have a problem and you had better dig deep and find some backbone somewhere.

Another thing to think about is when the dog doesn't do something straight away. If you tell the dog to sit and it plays about and then sits you have a dilemma, if you praise it the dog does not understand that you are praising it for the sit at the end, it thinks you are praising it for playing about and then sitting, the dog thinks you like this behaviour, so it's more likely that it will continue to play about and then sit. So you really do have to think about what you are saying to the dog, if you say 'good dog' when it isn't being a good dog you are telling the dog that you like it being naughty. You have to judge the praise according to how happy you are with what the dog has just done. If it carries out what you want in a prompt energetic manner then reward it with lots of praise/cuddles/titbits/play. If it eventually does what you want then okay just scale back the praise, you don't 'rip its legs off' - but if its work wasn't good enough it doesn't get a titbit. If it's done something that it <u>knows was naughty</u> then you have to make the dog understand that that wasn't a good idea and if it does the same thing again you will really get mad.

The reason that I've underlined <u>naughty</u> is that I want to emphasise that it's no good beating the dog up for something it doesn't understand, if it's a puppy and it pees on the carpet well hard luck the fault is yours for not taking it outside five minutes ago, secondly it might not have the bladder control to allow it to wait until it gets outside. If it's an older dog and it pees on the carpet then first thought should be that it might have a medical infection so it's not the dogs fault!

If the dog is of an age to know about titbits, and I wouldn't do this to a puppy, then there is nothing to stop you showing the dog the titbit that you have in your hand, and sadly putting it away if the dog's actions weren't good enough. Talking about titbits, it's quite normal for your dog to be willing to work in your garden for a grotty bit of old dog biscuit, but then handlers come to club and get surprised when the dog doesn't want the grotty bit of biscuit - it would far rather go off and play with the other dogs - you have to have something really tasty and attractive in such a situation, something like cheese, cooked meat, cold sausage works well.

I have mentioned 'ripping the dog's leg off' - I have never had to carry out this threat, I can't claim that this proves it works but it brings me to a thought. If you get to the point where you are starting to lose your temper then stop what you are doing, shut the dog away and cool down, you are not going to make any progress.

Second point, once the dog knows that it will survive 'having its legs ripped off' (assuming you are not a psychopath) you have nothing left to scare the dog with - you've lost.

At the risk of being sexist some people find it very difficult to talk to their dogs in a 'happy' voice, principally this is men, because their voice is lower in pitch it always sounds like they are crosser than they really are. Women have the other difficulty that because their voice is higher pitched they have difficulty sounding properly cross. If you are not sure how you sound to your dog, then ask someone else – if you truly sound cross or if you truly sound happy to that person, then there is a chance then your dog will also be convinced, and remember it doesn't actually matter what you say to your dog it's the way that you say it. On the down side women have a tendency to screech when they are trying to be cross – and that's not very impressive.

There is also the problem that some people always give an instruction in a strict voice as though the dog has done something wrong already – give the poor dog a chance, try a happy voice in the first instance, if it doesn't work you can always get heavy in the next instance. Hopefully the dog will soon work out that if he does what you ask first time then you won't use the harsh voice, but give him a chance before you get the harsh voice out, if he's going to get told off anyway he might just think he may as well do something naughty to deserve it.

12. A NICE PLACE TO BE

You've got to make your dog believe that being near to you is a really nice interesting place to be. If you take your dog for a walk up the woods then it may, at times, go further from you than you would like, make sure that when it comes beetling back to check out that you are coming then you are pleased to see him and tell him so, even if he goes rushing past in the opposite direction. It's probably more tempting to tell him off for going so far away, but if you do that then what you are you getting into his brain is 'I really want to go further than I know she likes, she'll only tell me off when I go back so I might as well stay a long way away for a long time so that she'll only tell me off the once.'

If when he does come rushing past you've got his tennis ball in your hand (assuming he's keen on balls) then he will start to think, 'bother I shouldn't have gone so far away because it would have been more interesting to play with the ball, and now she's put it in her pocket, I had better stay closer in case she gets it out again',

Or if you've got an old dog that stays with you then when the youngster is rushing back you give the old dog a treat, hopefully he'll think 'I should have stayed closer this is where all the treats are.'

I have to admit that this doesn't always work out the way you wanted, my youngster 'Kipper' is so keen on her ball that if I have it in my pocket she will not go further than five feet from my side, which is good in a way but not what I want when I'm just going for a walk. (I've since found out that if I put her ball in a plastic bag before putting it in my pocket then there is a good chance that she won't smell that I've got it.)

13. I DON'T CARE WHAT YOU DO – BUT DON'T DO THAT

There will be a time when your dog does something inappropriate, something you don't want him to do, supposing he steals your slipper, the temptation is to 'shout' at your dog and tell him off. Now look at things from your dog's point of view, he was minding his own business and being ignored by you, then just by chance he does something, and all of a sudden he gets a reaction from you – some attention, you may sound cross but this is better than being ignored, you're reacting.

So you chase him round the garden, snatch the slipper out of his mouth, tell him off, no way are you going to take him for a walk because you're cross with him. And the dog skulks off, and he's bored, but hold on, he now knows an interesting little diversion, he can steal something and all of a sudden he's got your attention!

Look at things another way supposing that, instead of shouting at him because he's got your slipper in his mouth, you call him to you – he won't come straight away because he doesn't know if you're cross with him, so you call him again, and he comes to you, and you can tell him truthfully that he's a very good boy for bringing the slipper.

You don't go overboard; you don't give him a treat. You don't want him to work out that whenever he wants a treat he's simply got to take something to you. Treats should be reserved for when you ask him to do something – not when he decides to do something.

Net result is that you get your slipper back before he chews it, you didn't have to chase him round the garden and then tell him off, so you are still in a good mood and happy. Dog learns that Mum is pleased that he took her slipper to her, but it wasn't very rewarding, he didn't get a titbit for it and he didn't get chased and Mother didn't lose her temper – probably it's not worth his while making a habit of taking her things. And remember, next time when you come in the house you can say 'fetch my slipper' and because he knows that you were okay when he had your slipper in his mouth last time. There's a chance that, although he doesn't know what you want but he knows you want something, he'll run around looking for something, with a bit of luck and a bit of encouragement from you, he'll find your slipper more by luck then judgement and pick it up. This time you'll be very pleased and encouraging when he does pick up your slipper and reward him for doing this. You've just taken the first step to having a helpful dog.

Although I would certainly go back to doing whatever it was that I was doing in the first place, I would also think to myself 'Why is the dog doing things like that?' Is it because he's got a point, and you've been doing other things for so long, and he's so bored and he really needs some attention and it is time for his walk anyway? Then, after you've made a show of doing whatever it was you were doing, you can decide to take the dog for a walk – so it's your choice not his, not a result of the dog picking up your slipper. If you straight away stop what you're doing and take him for a walk then you are rewarding him for stealing your property, and the behaviour is likely to be repeated.

A common complaint is people having dogs that jump up, now you can tell him not to and he'll probably stop doing it when he's aged about 24, or you can give him an alternative command before he starts jumping up, possibly 'sit' (presuming of course that he knows what the word means and will understand). Now it's simply not possible for the dog to jump up while he's sitting, so you can praise him madly for sitting when he was told, and praise him as well for not jumping up, the dog will sit there grinning inanely, he's got what he wanted, he only wanted to be given some attention after all. You've got a dog that will eventually realise that he actually gets more and better attention for doing a behaviour that you like, hopefully he will choose this behaviour for himself, you've only got to remember to make it worth his while, net result is the dog is happy and so are you!

So if your dog is doing something that you don't like, try and work out a behaviour that you would be happier with. So instead of just telling him something is bad, try and tell him what it is that you would rather he was doing. Hopefully this will end up with both you and the dog being happy!

14.   JUST BECAUSE YOU'RE DEAF?

Now it's a sad fact that of all the dogs that come to the training class some of them will end up deaf, and I mean deaf as in 'unable to hear anything' not just unable to hear things like 'come' and 'behave' but every time you take the lid of the biscuit tin he's heard and he's sitting waiting. So, while the dog is just at the start of his life, consider teaching him sign language <u>along</u> with the traditional vocal commands we use – you might think that this all sounds like extra work well it isn't really, because they are dogs and because dogs naturally spend all their lives 'reading' body language then this is something that comes to them very easily, all you have to do it to give them the signs along with the vocal command.

In addition, and this isn't really a valid reason for doing it, if, for example, you can command your dog to lie down with a signal while still continuing the conversation with someone else, then the someone else is often highly impressed.

I usually start with a sit, tell the dog to 'Sit' and hold your hand at an angle of 45 degrees, keep this up for a week or so, and then forget to say the command just hold your hand at an angle, you may well find that your dog sits anyway, if he doesn't then go back to using the vocal command and try again in a day or two. If he's still not getting it then make sure he knows that you've got a titbit for him, if he's got any brains then he'll sit quickly enough.

Later on you may well go on to teach him to stop and sit at a distance, if he knows to sit when he sees the hand at an angle then this is a relatively easy command, when he is at a distance from you then just hold the arm above shoulder height still at an angle of 45 degrees, accompany it with the vocal command and the dog soon learns.

Once he's sitting then you can try the command to lie down, this is simply holding the hand parallel with the ground, again start with the vocal command as well as the sign, most dogs cotton on very quickly.

When calling your dog to you hold your hands wide, (so you make the shape of the cross), this is a good visible signal, a lot of people make the mistake of holding their hands in front of them, but if your dog is a little way away and if the light is bad he won't be able to see the signal. If you have your dog out and the weather is bad and it's blowing a gale and your dog is over the other side of the field then you will have difficulty making him hear your call, so you'll be very grateful you've taught him this one.

Although there is actually just the one command to come in practical terms it means
- 'Come and sit in front of me'. Or
- 'You're a bit far away so just come a bit closer then carry on with what you're doing'

I originally make the sign to come, (arms wide) then I move both arms to point at the ground in front of me when I want him to come a sit in front of me or I just drop the sign when he's close enough so he knows that I'm happy with him being where he is.

You'll probably go on to develop signs of your own, and if your dog does go deaf then he'll already know the most useful and relevant signals anyway so it's a shame, but it's not the end of the world. This will also have the advantage that it makes it rewarding to look at you often, and this is something that should be encouraged.

My old dog, Ticket, went deaf as she got old. It wasn't a problem because she reacted so well to hand signals and the cues I gave her that it took quite some time for me to realise she was deaf.

15. GET DOWN SHEP!

Dogs jump up, if you're lucky it's small terriers, if you're unlucky its large muddy labradors and you could easily end in hospital. Now the reason they jump is huge and diversified, but they all have one thing in common - the dog is benefiting from jumping up.

Now that may seem strange when you immediately tell them they are naughty and to get down, but look at it from the dogs point of view HE GOT NOTICED - and that's often better than not being noticed. You can spend the next fifteen years telling the dog off, but that's boring. Also consider - if you have to tell the dog off for the next fifteen years it actually confirms that the dog hasn't learnt anything because the dog does not change its behaviour. If you're old enough to remember the origin of the phrase 'get down Shep' (John Noakes on Blue Peter) you can think about it, and the fact he had to repeat it for ten years or so only goes to prove that it didn't work to change the dog's behaviour!

So, to make the dog want to change his behaviour it's up to you to think things through. Why is the dog jumping up, is it because you've just returned and he's pleased to see you and he wants to get noticed, (alternatively is it because he's been digging in the flower bed and he wants to show you how muddy he is? Oh you've just noticed and it's all over your clothes). It will also make the change of behaviour much much much quicker if you tell the dog what alternative behaviour to do which is going to please you much more.
e.g. you come in and he's really pleased to see you and jumps all over you, alternative behaviour is for him to sit in his bed with his bum on the floor and you go over to his bed and praise him.

So you've got to persuade him that it's really unrewarding for him to jump up. By telling him off you are actually giving him a reward because you are speaking him, just suppose that you give him the 'freeze' treatment instead, turn your back and pretend he's invisible, but you just happen to sidle across the room to his bed, and you just happen to indicate to him to get in the bed, and you whisper the magic word 'sit' and he does, and suddenly he's visible again, and you talk to him, and praise him, and take a titbit out of the jar that you just happened to leave handy but out of his reach - and of course while he's sitting it's not possible for him to jump up.

In not very many repetitions your dog has learnt that while jumping up may be fun, a more rewarding choice is to go and sit in his bed, because then you'll be so pleased you'll praise him and reward him and it will be even better. A word of warning and a caution here. While it is easy (comparatively) to train the dog, a far harder task is to train all the visitors that come to your house, a lot of people actually like being jumped up at and say things like 'oh I don't mind,' and they encourage your dog to continue. I fully understand if you say through gritted teeth 'well he's my dog and I do mind', but do you want to have a row with all your visitors? Consider, if you say you've been told not to let the dog jump up because his back might be a bit suspect, this often works to make visitors not encourage bad behaviour, I know the visitor will assume the vet said it, so you don't have to explain it was someone advising on dog training and she tells lies anyway.

This is one scenario, there are many, but they all have the same principles. You have to work out how the dog is benefiting from jumping up and give him an alternative and better behaviour and reward him for making the 'correct' choice!

16. SEXUAL DISCRIMINATION

Now at the risk of being politically incorrect, I've got to say there are advantages in being male and female - apart from the obvious ones. Men have naturally deep gruff voices, women have higher pitched voices. Men are great at telling dogs off, women are great at telling the dog he's done right.

Often when you listen to a woman telling off dogs (or kids) you will hear a sort of high pitched screeching, sometimes when you listen to a man saying 'good dog' he uses the same tone of voice as he uses when his football team has just lost the cup final.

Men who want the dog to understand that the dog has just done something right and he's a really good boy will get a much better reaction if they put on a 'silly' high pitched girly voice. Women who just discover their dog has done something naughty (not yours obviously) have to lower the voice and speak sternly.

It really does work better, you will get strange looks if you're out in public but your dog is more important than your dignity.

17. 'I CAN'T TELL THE DOG OFF BECAUSE IF I DO IT WON'T LOVE ME'

It will love you more if it believes that you are a strong active 'pack leader'. If it thinks that you are a totally incompetent pushover then the dog will think that he, the dog, has to be pack leader -and because the dog is only ever a dog it will not understand things like humans going off to work, driving a car, visitors coming to the house, policeman, the Dangerous Dogs Act. The list is endless. Dogs make rotten pack leaders in a human world, the dog will be living under unimagined stress, but if the dog is living in a happy pack with a strong pack leader then its life will be much happier.

The job of a pack leader –
   a. Discipline
   b. Exercise
   c. Appropriate food and water

           And lastly

   d. Affection

   Probably in that order of importance, and 'affection' means supplying the previous three in the list, it doesn't mean an endless supply of chocolate biscuits, tins of Doggydins and cuddles on the sofa to replace the discipline, exercise, and appropriate food and water that you should be supplying.

18. FIREWORKS

Now personally I would affix anyone setting off fireworks to their own rockets, well okay, they can do it for two hours on November 5th. But Fireworks are something we have to put up with, and how you react can have a huge impact to how your dog reacts for the rest of his life.

Exercise the dog well in the daylight, feed him well, they'll sleep better. Then draw the curtains, put on the telly loud and settle down for the night. When fireworks start going off you <u>CANNOT</u> reassure your dog by petting it or giving it titbits – your dog will interpret this as you rewarding him for being scared! Next time he hears fireworks he will act scared because he thinks he will be rewarded again. The only way you reassure your dog is by showing him that you are not scared! You can 'be impressed' by really big bangs, some dogs actually seem to enjoy them, but do not give him consolation for being scared.

It's a sad fact that some dogs are scared whatever you do, you can build them a sanctuary by making a small little 'cave' which is only just big enough for the dog, a sheltered dark spot behind the sofa, or under the bed or under the table, sheltered by cushions or such like so at least the dog can hide himself away. You might just find that when he realises that you aren't frightened he'll come out looking embarrassed.

If you have to let the dog out in the garden for a pee and if your garden is not guaranteed very escape proof then take your dog out on a lead, because it is almost inevitable that a firework will go off while you are out there. Do not take chances because your dog is okay every other night, make sure he is wearing a collar and an identification tag. Remember, once the fireworks appear in the shops it is not only 5th November that is a problem, it is the week beforehand, the week after, every weekend until Christmas, especially bad on New Year, and then hopefully the shops will have sold all their sparklers!

This probably also applies to thunder and lightning, except you can't blame anyone for it apart from possibly God of course, and some dogs are also scared of the sound of shotguns but you can probably choose to go elsewhere when they're about.

46

19. FETCH

Life's fun if your dog knows how to fetch a ball and, being purely practical, you can get your dog to do a lot of exercise without moving very far at all. But there are some things which ought to be thought of.

It's very easy to pick up a stick and throw it, but there are a lot of dogs which have ended up at the vets when the stick has bounced wrongly and got stuck in its throat point first – not nice, and being purely practical, expensive as well, and I'm sure that some dogs haven't lived long enough to come home from the vets. I don't throw sticks, it's up to you, and it's your dog. People throw balls, Frisbees, fluffy toys, slippers, kongs, gun dog dummies, and many other things. What you have to be careful of is only throwing a ball that is sufficiently large that it can't get stuck in the dog's throat and suffocate him. Not nice. I won't use golf balls, they're the wrong size for my sort of dogs, tennis ball size is okay but if you've got a very large dog then they might be a bit risky.

Just consider, if you hope to have your dog for the next ten to fifteen years then the novelty of bending down to pick a ball off the ground is going to fade, there's absolutely no reason why your dog can't learn to put things in your hand. Once the dog realises that the only way to get his ball thrown is if he puts it in your hand then he will very soon learn to put in your hand, if he throws it on the floor in front of you then leave it there or pick it up and put it away! Plus, if you go on to train your dog further he will be doing a conventional retrieve when the dog has to sit in front of you with the retrieve in his mouth – this will be considerably easier if he knows to hold something until you take it.

Once your dog learns that you might just have his ball with you then life gets more interesting for him. There's nothing to stop you going for a walk and having the ball in your pocket, the dog is more likely to want to hang around you if there's potentially something exciting happening. You can actually take the ball out and hold it in your hand, or toss it up in the air and play with it on your own if the dog persists in going off too far. The rule is, if your dog is too far away then he misses out on playing the game with you - occasionally you have to work it so the dog is close enough to play the game with you, he's got to learn the benefits of being close.

A problem that some people have is that they can't get the ball out of the dog's mouth, this is just boring, but look at it from the dog's point of view, he's got this terrific toy and you're trying to steal it off him! It's fun to hang on to it tightly.

What you've got to teach the dog is that if he gives it up then something even better happens, maybe you'll throw it again, maybe you'll give him a titbit and then give him the ball back, maybe you'll give him an even better toy. <u>So there ends up being no reason for him to fight you for it.</u> It's worth having a command which means 'give it to me now' if your dog knows that 'give' or 'dead' or whatever you use means give it up this instant then you can go on to play 'tuggy' games with him - when you pull on something when he's got hold of one end.

A word of warning here, if you've got the sort of dog that gets very excited by this sort of game, it should only be played if, when you command your dog to 'give' at any point, he will stop and give you the toy, if he goes over the top then you are leading into a situation that could be aggressive and it will end in tears. Be careful if you've got smallish children – the dog may win and you don't want him to learn that he's stronger than the children. Also, it's not a game that you play with a dog that will grow up to be a gun dog.

If you are having trouble taking the item out of your dog's mouth then make sure you are using things that are big enough, and sticks out of the mouth and gives you something to take hold of. When you've got hold of it don't try and pull it out of the mouth, this will only encourage the dog to grip harder. Rotate the item instead, hopefully this will be unexpected and the dog will still be relaxed and will release the item, thus he gives it up, you get really pleased and give him a titbit and <u>then give him the item back</u>.

(I offer this information with the admission I've never tried it and don't necessarily recommend it. I heard a gun dog trainer state that to get the dog to give up the item then you blow up the dog's nose! Now I don't know that I want to go around blowing up strange dogs noses, in my opinion it puts you a bit close to their teeth, but if you know the dog then it's worth considering.)

If you're going to continue attending training classes then you will (hopefully) be learning the conventional retrieve, now the tricky thing for some dogs is that they've got to sit and wait while the item is thrown and only go and fetch it when they are told. Really keen dogs find this difficult, especially really keen gun dog breeds that have been allowed to run after the retrieve straight away, will struggle with this one. So it's worth considering teaching your dog early to wait until he gets the command to go and fetch.

You might think that this is petty, but suppose you've just thrown something for your dog to fetch and a very large ferocious looking Rottweiler (or something similar) decides to go and fetch it instead – now it might be cowardice, but I'm happy to let discretion be the better part of valour I don't want my dog fighting the Rotty for it. Or suppose you throw something and it bounces wrong and lands in the road and there's a car coming!

What we want to emphasise to the dog is that he hasn't got a right to go and fetch everything, he only goes if you let him, after all, you are the boss!   It enhances your relationship with the dog if you are able to have a game of fetch with him, and it raises the dog's opinion of you as being the provider of wonderful things like balls. Being purely practical, there will be occasions when you simply won't have the time to walk as much as he needs, if the dog spends fifteen minutes galloping after a retrieve he will use up a lot more energy – but, if you've got a puppy or a young dog remember that it's not a good idea for him to get too tired or you will get joint and skeletal problems arising, (and keep an eye on the kids if they are out playing with him).

Consider, rather than just letting him run blindly after a ball that he saw, drop the ball without the dog seeing, walk on ten yards (or metres if you walk in metric) and then tell him you've lost something, I usually do this by holding up my empty hands, although he will be confused at first and just run around, because you haven't gone too far from the ball he will eventually fall over it and bring it to you, you'll be very pleased and reward him. Once he's got the idea you can gradually increase the distance until he's having to go back a considerable way.

A step on from this is to sit the dog, throw the ball twenty foot, bend down so your arm is near the dogs eye level and point your arm at the ball and then send him, repeat this a few times and hopefully your dog will learn that it is worth going in the direction that you are pointing. Once you think he's twigged, throw the ball without the dog seeing, bring him back to you, and then send the dog for the ball by pointing in the direction you want him to go and giving him the verbal command 'fetch' which he should know by now. He won't understand. But he should go in the right direction anyway because that's where you've pointed, and he should find the ball. Once it's understood, it's simply a case of increasing the distance gradually.

20. NOW THAT YOUR DOG IS GOOD AND WORTH STEALING

I wish there was nothing to write here, but it's a sad fact that it does happen. I would certainly recommend that you have your dog protected in some way and I suppose I'm thinking of microchip or tattoo or possibly both, but I've just read an article that links microchips to cancer so I think I would have to check that out before my next dog.

Naturally you will take lots of photos of your dog anyway but it would make sense to take the sort of photo that you could use on a missing dog poster, I hope that you never have to use it.

21. DEFINITELY NOT GOOD FOR YOUR DOG

Sadly, there are things that we eat and use that will quite easily (and sometimes rapidly) kill your dog. Possibly the most common of these is human chocolate and unfortunately has the sort of taste that will mean that a lot of dogs will steal it if they find it unattended. A taste will probably not kill your dog unless you have a very small dog, not that I'm recommending it of course, but if your dog gets hold of any quantity of chocolate then it is a serious matter and veterinary opinion should be sought promptly. This is an excellent excuse not to share your chocolates with your dog!

Anti-freeze is another potential killer, not that you would deliberately give some to your dog, but apparently it tastes sweet and they will readily polish if off if they find some available, and do-it-yourself mechanics have been known to drain out anti-freeze and leave it in an open container.

Raisins, grapes, currants and sultanas are not good for dogs – again a taste will probably not harm, but some dogs will be tempted to steal if they are able to, and that might cause harm.

Xylitol is a substance used to sweeten amongst other things, sugar free chewing gum, at the moment there is no antidote and it doesn't need a lot to kill.

Slug killer and poisons you use in the gardens are obvious things to avoid although some of the advertising suggests that dogs will not choose to eat them, history relates that dogs have eaten them and subsequently died. Great care should be taken in their use, and be especially vigilant if you visit strange gardens which aren't used to having dogs about.

22. NO! NO! NO! = YES! YES! YES!

People are very willing to tell the dog 'NO' whenever it does something wrong, or thinks about doing something wrong, what I want to point out is that if you are willing to say 'no' when it does something wrong, then it is a very good idea if you say ' yes' when your dog is learning to do something new and he doesn't really know what you want – if you say 'yes' (preferably in a pleased happy voice) then the dog will get the idea that you're pleased with what he's doing – at this point he doesn't understand but you're telling him that what he is doing is right and to carry on doing it!

Incidentally, if your dog is learning something new (with the exception of the recall) then don't make the mistake of using his name! His name means stop what you're doing and come to me, if you are trying to teach the dog to stay and you say 'Fido stay' then you are actually saying 'come here I love you, but stay where you are' - no wonder the poor dog is confused!

Another thing, if you are teaching something like the recall, and you tell your dog to sit and then you get a really tasty treat out of your pocket and wave it under his nose, but then you walk away how much more tempting is it for your dog to follow you for the treat. Tell your dog to sit, then walk away and at the same time get the treat out of your pocket.

I have noticed that some people when practising the recall walk away really, really slowly believing that this makes the dog more likely to stay. This doesn't work, the dog is most likely to stay for - say ten seconds, if you have walked away at a normal unexciting pace and then called him after ten seconds the chances are that he will still be sitting there - but just thinking of getting up – if you are moving at snail's pace then after ten seconds you'll only be two foot away and three foot when he gets up and comes after you. In situation one you have success, you can praise him and reward him, and the next time, because he was praised after the first time, he'll sit there for fifteen seconds!

23. YOU HAVE TO RECOGNISE WHO CONTROLS THE TREATS

I love training with rewards, I'm a great believer in bribery and corruption, but if you're not careful you can fall into a situation when the dog will only do something if you've got a treat in your hand. Now for the first few times of learning something it's a great idea if the dog is working for a treat, but once he understands the situation then it is important that he should act willingly in the hope he'll get the treat anyway.

A typical situation is teaching the dog to lie down, it's great to use a treat to get him to lie, but once he understands what is happening then if you use the hand movement that you used when you had the treat ready, you will probably find he lies down expecting the treat is in the hand, at which point you can produce the treat from your pocket and give it to him. Very soon he will recognise the verbal command (which of course you've been using) and you can use less and less of a hand signal, once he's got good at this, you can only use a treat to reward the very best lie downs.

While we're on the subject of food treats let me just explain what I'm talking about. I mean the smallest possible amount of the least tasty thing that he will work for. At home, when it's perfectly boring anyway, this might mean a fraction of a dog biscuit, at club when there are lots of other dogs about he might tell you, in the nicest possible way, what you can do with his fraction of a dog biscuit, but a piece of cheese or a bit of cooked meat, or a slice of sausage, well that's a different matter. You know your dog better than I do, you'll have to be willing to experiment.

If you are worried about your dog getting fat well, don't panic. If you are teaching a new behaviour and using lots of treats then just give him less food at meal times. If you are bringing him to a club and you want him to be keen on his treats well, don't give him his evening meal until he gets home.

24. I DON'T LIKE WRITING THIS - But

I wish I didn't feel obliged to write this, and I'm not knocking your vets, but I'm just asking you to think about something. The trainee vets go to vets school, where they are educated at vast expense by colleges that are grateful to receive funding from the Companies that make a lot of money from manufacturing veterinary drugs. Now funnily enough the colleges are not going to upset the companies that are giving them the money, and if the companies say things like 'dogs have to be vaccinated every year' this is what they teach the people who go on to become vets and repeat the same information to their clients. There is no truly independent research into whether or not these vaccinations are actually needed.

A further consideration is what happens if a dog has an adverse reaction following an injection, this gets reported back to the company who made the vaccination, who mostly concludes that this had no relation to the recent vaccination. There is no <u>independent</u> body to examine the facts. You may live many decades vaccinating your dog every year, but if your dog develops cancer - for instance, or neurological problems, or paralysis, or hair loss, or skin problems, then you will be more than a little upset.

There is an organisation called Canine Health Concern which is totally independent but runs on a shoestring. They have a very good web site and the true stories they relate are scary. If you have an hour or two to spare have a look at their site and then consider whether what your vet tells you is truly independent and worthwhile advice.

In the USA they inject into the top of the dogs hind leg - because if the dog develops a reaction to the injection they can amputate the leg and the dog lives! I'm not sure that I want my vet to use something that is so risky that it had to go into some part of the animal that is removable.

While we're on the subject, there is a lot of publicity about feeding your dog a raw and natural diet, bones and all. I don't, mainly because I'm too lazy and it sounds like extra work, but I do attempt to feed a 'good quality' dog food, which isn't the cheapest.

A true story, many years ago I worked with a girl whose father was a huntsman, now hunts feed dead animals, which is great, but when the bones were chewed up, played with and discarded by the hounds then a big lorry would come to take them away to be used in the manufacture of a very well known and well advertised dog food!   I don't wish to feed my dogs something which other dogs leave.

25. FOUR LEGS AND AN ENGINE

It's very hard to manage these days without a car, and if you choose to then you're a better person than I am, and if you've got both a car and a dog then it's inevitable that it'll make your life better if they mix together happily.

Every year there is at least one report on the news that a dog has suffocated in a car. Half of me says lynch the person responsible, and the other half feels so much sorrow for them because they will always feel guilty about it. It is a fact that cars get hot even in relatively warmish weather, if you are hoping/intending to leave your dog in the car then stop the vehicle, wind the windows up to the level that you intend to leave the dog in the car with   AND JUST SIT THERE FOR FIVE MINUTES! If it's getting unpleasant and you want to wind down the window then there is no way it is safe to leave the dog in the car, he can't wind down the window - he will just die and surprisingly quickly in some cases. If it's pleasant in the car and you're happy to leave the dog, and he's got some drinking water handy, then just think about how long you are going to be gone, while the car might be adequately shaded at the moment then just think that the sun will move and may be full on the car in an hour or so.

If you've got a hatchback then there is a little gadget you can buy that will let you leave the hatch open slightly, but will still let you lock the car! This has the advantage that fresh air is entering the car at the dog's level if it is lying down, but the dog is still secure. It's called a Vent-lock, but there are probably other makes called other things, and you should find it on the internet. It's worth investigating.

There are two common problems with dogs in cars, they either love them or they hate them. Both problems are often caused by handlers!

Dogs that hate cars are fetched in them as puppies, they are nervous, scared, and usually manage to be sick. They are then put in the car again to go to the vet for the injection, and again for the follow up, any wonder he's starting not to like cars - every time he gets in one he's sick or he gets injected! So the owner is now ready to take him places, but he doesn't like the car and he's car sick, so they leave him for a few months thinking it will magically go away on its own, but it doesn't. So they end up with a dog that is really nervous about going in the car, so they leave the dog at home rather than force the issue and owning a dog is not as much fun as they thought it would be.

There's the other end of the scale of course, the dogs that are so excited about going in the car that they bounce around all over the place. They only go in the car when they are going somewhere exciting for a walk, they whine and dribble and bark at everyone they go past, this is so boring!

What you've got to achieve is a happy medium, if you've got a 'hyped' up sort then you've got to put him in the car so often just to drive to the garage, to the shops, anywhere that is really boring that the dog concludes it's not worth getting excited about. If you've got the nervous sort then you've got to give him lot's of short rewarding trips, so that a car journey means going somewhere for a walk, so that it is worth putting up with the car because it will end with something exciting.

<u>Be careful</u>. Trips have to be short to start with, very short, possibly just the length of the drive, the street, two streets, so that the dog survives the trip without being car sick, so that it can get out of the car with you being very pleased with it. Build things up gradually!

If your dog keeps being car sick then explore remedies, feed it before, feed it after, let it travel on the floor, in a cage, in a covered cage. One chap spent nearly a year (and a lot of money) trying to stop his dog being sick, then following an accident he hired a car for a fortnight, and the dog was perfectly alright. When he got his own car back and it was sick again, he investigated further and discovered that there was a slight leak of fumes blowing back just where the dog sat – no wonder it was sick. But whatever you do, don't avoid the dog being sick by avoiding the car, however well it works in the short term things will change and you'll still have the problem.

Owning a dog does not mix well with having a smart clean polished car - personally I'm not that interested in having a smart clean car. A dog also does not mix with locking up your car securely with all the windows wound up when you leave the car. This is a problem you have to come to terms with before buying your dog.

A word of the highest importance – your dog must <u>not</u> learn that as soon as the car door is open he can jump out, this might seem of trifling importance to you now, but one day you will break down on the motorway or somewhere similar, open a door to get something and your dog will jump out, and there will be a big splat as a lorry goes by. Your dog must learn to stay in the car even though the door is open and until you give him the word that tells him it is permissible to get out!

Another word of warning, dogs often sit in the car quite happily, but beware, the dog may consider that the car is his territory, and if someone sticks their hand in the window to stroke the dog he may just defend his territory very aggressively. People should not attempt to touch other people's dogs which are in cars, even if they think they know the dog, they might just lose their fingers which is bad enough. What is even worse is that if your dog does attack someone while he is in the car he is judged to be on public property, you can be prosecuted and he can be destroyed.

Incidentally, because he is judged to be on public property in a car he should by law be wearing his collar with a tag giving his owner's name and address.

It's very boring owning a dog that thinks it's incapable of jumping into the car. Your dog should like going in the car, and he should be happy to jump in. If it's too small physically then obviously you'll have to lift him in, if it's old, infirm, or ailing then you'll have to struggle and lift him, or buy a ramp, or find a box he can climb on, but if it's young and fit and perfectly capable of jumping then you've got to be a bit devious. It's very tempting to give him a good kick up the …. But that probably isn't going to do a lot of good in the long run, a better solution is to perhaps find his favourite toy, wind the dog up a bit, and then throw the toy into the car, hopefully he'll jump in. Or keep some treats in a dog proof container in the car, as soon as he gets in he can have one - bribery is a wonderful thing. Possibly the dog is just lacking a bit of confidence, so try giving him a step to make it easier for him, when that works swop the step for a smaller step, when he can cope with this, then take the step away.

If you get to the point where the dog is just refusing to try, (you will of course have had him vet checked to make sure he is capable), then perhaps consider you could get in the car and slowly drive away, when the dog realises that you are going to go without him if he doesn't get in then he might just change his mind. Of course I'm only recommending this if you've got somewhere safe to do it, it definitely won't work it you drive over the dog on the way!

Another thing that I'm not recommending - I used to own wonderful springer spaniel called Tacit that would sit in the car quietly and happily for extremely long journeys, but then she would wake up, and if we drove past a dog walking on the pavement she would bark ferociously. I would nearly jump out of the car with the shock of it because I thought she was still asleep; this was the only time she would act ferocious, she used to get beaten up by small puppies. I put up with this for many years, but she did it once too often and I actually stopped the car (it was a very quiet place) and opened the door, she didn't want to get out, I virtually dragged her out, as soon as I let go of the collar she was back in the car and pretending to the be fast asleep and she didn't want to talk to the dog she had barked at, she never did it again.

26. THE BIGGER PICTURE

It's unfortunate, but it's the bigger picture that your dog looks at when he considers his position in the pack. (The pack = your household and all the people living in it.)

He might be brilliant at things like recall, sitting when he's told, not attacking your small child, but overall he may consider, rightly, that really you're not much of a pack leader. You might leap to your feet when he says it's time to feed him, you might wander along on a walk allowing him to sniff at ALL the interesting smells, and you might cuddle him every time he says he wants a cuddle. What all these things are telling him is that you're not taking control very efficiently – and, because (in the dog world) every pack MUST have a pack leader and you're not filling the position then, he will have to be pack leader.

You may think 'so what' at this point, but just consider when he goes out in the garden and digs up the plants you've just spent a small fortune buying and then he places it covered in mud in the middle of the carpet, then naturally you'll tell him off – and he will think to himself 'why is this lesser pack member telling me off? I'm the boss here, I'll take no notice'. You may as well save your breath!

Now you might argue that it's because I love him so that I let him be the pack leader, but are you sure that is in his best interest? There are going to be times when you need to go out and leave him home alone, now this is extremely stressful for a pack leader who hasn't got a clue where the rest of the pack has gone, what they're doing, and when, if ever, they're coming back. People come to the front door and ring the bell, he hasn't got a clue who they are and what they want, but he knows that he has to protect his pack so probably the safest thing to do is to bark like mad until they go away – and you wonder why your friends don't visit often!

So just look at your life with your dog, and think about who <u>your dog</u> thinks is in charge and just consider whether you do things because your dog thinks this is what you should do or because it is what you think you should do. And just possibly, think about insisting that he does things that you ask him to do before he gets to do the nice things that he wants to do.

27. HOW MANY DOGS DOES IT TAKE TO CHANGE A LIGHT BULB?

Golden Retriever	The sun is shining the day is young, but you're inside worried about a light bulb?
Border Collie	Just this one, and then I'll replace any wiring that doesn't comply with the regulations
Dachshund	You know I can't reach that stupid lamp
Rottweiler	Make me!

Labrador	Oh me, me please let me. Can I? Can I? Huh huh huh can I?
German Shepherd	I'll change it as soon as I've led these people from the dark, checked to make sure I haven't missed anyone and made just one more patrol to see no one has tried to take advantage of the situation.
Poodle	If I blow in the Border Collie's ear he'll do it. By the time he's finished rewiring my nails will be dry
Maltese	Let the Border Collie do it, you can feed me while he's busy
Jack Russell	I'll just pop it in while I'm bouncing of the walls and furniture
Cocker Spaniel	Why change it? I can still pee on the carpet in the dark
Greyhound	It isn't moving so what's the point?
Old English Sheepdog	Light Bulb, I'm sorry but I don't see a light bulb
Newfoundland	Why would you want to do that? The light at the end of my tunnel has never worked and I don't have a problem

28. ON THE LEAD - OR THE HARNESS - OR THE HALTI - OR WHAT?

Now I've already admitted I'm lazy, I don't want to spend ten minutes putting on gadgets before I go for a walk. I use a rope slip lead - and if you don't know it, that's basically a rope with a ring on the end, and you make the end into the loop that goes over the dog's head, and you can take it off and shove it in a pocket, and you can tie it in a knot and play fetch with it, but that's a different story, and you can tie up fences and even catch escaped horses with it but that's another different story.

My dogs all wear a collar which has a tag on it giving my address (that's a legal requirement by the way). Just because it works for me I am not trying to insist that you use the same. Basically you can use whatever you like (excluding a pinch collar and a remote control shock collar in my training classes). There's a good argument for using a head collar if you are having trouble teaching your dog to walk at heel, especially if your dog is bigger and stronger than you - this works on the principle that you take control of the head and it is a lot harder for the dog to pull. There are a lot of different types on the market and because I have not used them all I cannot and will not recommend a particular brand - basically the right one to use is the one that works.

What I will put money on is that if you use a gadget then your dog won't like it at first, and the reason is that it gives you greater control over him. So you've got to introduce one with a great deal of tact, put it on and give him a tit bit etc. Because, hopefully, he won't spend the rest of his life in one, a great thing to do is to put a lead on the head collar, and a lead on his collar, and if he's pulling you can control him with the lead on the head collar, and if he's walking quietly and nicely you can use the lead that is on his collar. Hopefully he will work out for himself that it's to his benefit to walk quietly so you only use the lead on his collar, and eventually you can put the head collar in your pocket (just in case) and eventually forget it completely.

I have never used a harness, but if it works for you then I'm not knocking it. Because I've worked in the past with driving horses I've seen horses put in very similar arrangements to enable them to pull a carriage, so I really can't convince myself of their merits.

Choke chains have been rechristened check chains and you don't see them used so often. I don't recommend them but neither do I tell people they shouldn't use them, they have got a purpose. Half check chains are a kinder more modern equivalent, some people like them - I've never used one. What is nice is a simple, reasonably broad, collar.

A word of warning, if your collar or lead gets old and frayed then it is to be expected that it will break at the very worst moment, don't risk it, go out and buy a new one.

Pet shops are keen to sell you an extending lead - the sort where you can press a button and the lead gets longer and longer. Think about this from the dog's point of view, he's going along and he pulls and he gets rewarded by the lead getting longer, so you can't really blame the dog if he carries on pulling, all the work that you've done at getting the dog not to pull is getting undone! I don't use them, although I can see their worth if the dog is recovering from an operation and has to stay on the lead.

I was once sat in my car waiting for the traffic lights to change when a girl (I would guess she was aged about 12 to 14) came running down the road with a dog on an extended lead running with her, the lead was about 20' long at this stage. Girl ran left around a corner, dog didn't realise and went running across the road straight ahead. It was pure luck there was no car coming because the dog wouldn't have stood a chance. I don't like extending leads.

At club, if you've got a big bouncy dog who is used to a head collar, by all means bring him in wearing the head collar, work him in it until he settles down, then there will be a time when he realises that he isn't going anywhere, so try moving the lead so it's attached to his collar.

Pet shops and vets are keen that you spend money on a 'gadget' and they will tell you this will cure all the ills of the world, just bear in mind that they are making money on the gadgets you are buying so they might well be a bit biased!

29.   TURN THE TELLY UP, THERE'S SOMETHING GOOD ON.

Now some dogs never ever pay interest to what comes on the telly; some dogs like to yodel along with the soap opera tunes and some dogs get very excited when a regular programme ends. Think about it, if you watch something regularly and you regularly take them out for a walk after the programme, and then the music is a signal they are going out for a walk. Alas some dogs get very excited when they hear a programme that has a dog barking on it, this can be very very boring when they insist on barking back.

Now there are three ways of dealing with this. You can stick your fingers in your ears or turn the telly up and deal with the neighbours when they come round to complain. You can avoid watching 'doggy' programmes on the telly for the next ten years. Well yes, that's one way, but it's your telly not the dog's and you have to pay for the TV licence not him so why shouldn't you watch what you want, or you can attempt to deal with the problem. Or, I suppose, there's another way you can kick your dog out in the garden when the doggy programme is on, but perhaps we'll keep this as plan B.

You've got to look at things from your dog's point of view. He's sitting there quietly, probably dreaming of bones and rabbits and nice smells to roll in, then all of a sudden this peculiar box in the corner starts barking, possibly in an aggressive tone of voice, so is it any wonder he starts barking back. You know what the telly is and you know it isn't aggressive, but the dog thinks he's possibly saving the pack from threat and being a hero.

So, let's use modern technology, record lots of 'barking' programmes and when you've got them on the video, and don't really care about watching them so you're not going to be upset if he barks, and you know that your neighbours are out so they're not going to get upset, put the telly on quietly and let the dog hear the barking, but quietly, so he knows there's not a dog in there that's going to attack him. Your dog will probably listen and cock his ears, he'll possibly bark once or twice, but WHEN HE SHUTS UP AND IS QUIET you could give him one of the little treats that you just happen to have by your side. He'll probably ignore the telly and be more interested in you, so you can turn the telly up a little louder and because he's still more interested in your titbits you can reward him again for ignoring the TV.. Sometime later you'll probably turn the telly up and he'll just have to go and bark back, so you can tell him that you don't like this behaviour and you can put the treat away. If you're being really nice to him and letting him sit next to you on the sofa or cuddling him you can withdraw your affection so that he works out that if he barks back Mum doesn't like it and furthermore the dog doesn't like the results.

It probably shouldn't take too long, but if you stop watching 'barking' programmes then your dog will never ever get over it and you will be condemned to a lifetime of watching sport or something safe (or taking your dog for a walk which is far more fun anyway).

30. SEX

Well at least with a word like that I've got your attention! And this section isn't going to be particularly rude, so please don't skip it for fear of being offended. Sex is the most important thing to any species, without it that species is not going to continue so it is terrifically important to any animal that if they have the chance to reproduce they do so.

Whether or not you spay or castrate your dog, you've got to at least think about things.

If you've intend to have a litter of puppies then obviously you will do nothing initially. I have never produced puppies because I would have great difficulty finding homes for them, hopefully not because people wouldn't want them but because I would have impossibly unrealistically high standards before I would let the puppies go.

If you aren't going to have a litter from a bitch then you have seriously got to think about spaying her. Bitches in season are messy, anti-social and basically a pain to have around; spaying them takes away all those problems - the anxiety of male dogs doing the evil deed on the quiet, the implications of hormones coursing around the body and the potential future medical problems.

There are lots of people who have entire male dogs and never have any problems, (possibly if their dogs were human they would be carrying handbags), there are lots of people who have entire male dogs that are a pain but the husband in the family swears blind that he will never ever have him castrated - this is a 'male' thing. What you've got to consider is that although your animal is still entire you will never ever let him have sex! (And we're talking about the dog here not the husband). This is like being given a flashy red sports car but never being allowed to take it out of the garage, not a lot of fun once the novelty wears off and some people talk about letting the dog have sex once before you castrate him, this is a bit like taking the car out of the garage once, finding it's terrific fun, but never letting him drive it again. Also remember that a male dog can smell a bitch in season from a distance of two miles - how frustrating is that for him! I'm not saying that a castrated male cannot smell the same bitch but at least he won't care about it.

Another thing to think about is that I'm sure that you believe your dog is wonderful and well worth siring a litter or two, but if you owned a bitch that you wanted to breed from would you choose a reasonably handsome dog that happened to live up the next street – or would you go for a dog with a proven very good pedigree and a history of being shown or worked as appropriate. I know if I was buying a puppy I would want one sired by something with a good history.

So when you are outside with your dog off the lead and you call your dog, just at the moment a pretty little bitch walks past, is your dog going to come when he's called, or is he going to check out this canine vision of loveliness in the hope she's in season and wants his attention? What's going to work best, her flirtatious intentions or you standing there with a choccy drop in your hand calling like mad even if you get mad and threaten a beating then a lot of dogs will fall for the canine temptress and later happily accept the beating with a smile on his face.

And don't think that you will only have a problem when female dogs are about – if your dog is entire then he will have more instincts to be pack leader. This may involve dominating (beating up) other male dogs which might not make you popular down the park.

We have had a fair few entire dogs at the training class that have done well when they were younger. They have progressed and are working well off the lead when suddenly they realise that there is something more exciting than doing what is asked in class and they would rather go and sniff the other dogs! Sadly because the owners are not aware enough to insist, it's ended up with them not coming any longer.

I am not telling you to have your dog castrated or spayed, please don't do what I or anyone else tells you. All I am telling you is to think about whether or not you ought to have your dog castrated or spayed, and if you are happy to live with the consequences.

31. LANGUAGE PROBLEMS

Now you may think that it is inherent in dogs that they all talk the same language, but I don't think they do. Sometimes they go through phases in their lives when they learn to say something that works, then they go through their life saying the wrong thing in the wrong way and using language that totally upsets their owners.

Now you'll be wondering what on earth I'm on about, thinking what a lot of tosh, and you probably own a dog that you have owned since it was a puppy and that dog has absolutely no trouble meeting strangers and thinks that the whole world loves it. Aren't you lucky! Think of things another way, you do your bit and decide to take a dog from a rescue centre and the dog has, through no fault of his own, been taken away from his owners and dumped with a lot of strangers in a very scary rescue centre. Along comes another dog and because your dog has no idea what's going on it's shouted (barked) at the stranger to go away and unfortunately the stranger did, and your dog has thought 'well that's obviously the best way to deal with danger - bark until it goes away' and if the stranger doesn't go then it learns to bear his teeth or possibly bite. This is learned behaviour - IT DOES NOT USUALLY MEAN THAT THE DOG IS INHERENTLY NASTY.

Now there are at least two possible outcomes,

1. Along comes a new owner and takes the dog home. The dog barks at another dog in the park; the owner gets nervous and tense; doesn't let the dog off the lead because he's scared of what it might do and the dog recognises owner is nervous and tense every time they see another dog. So the dog thinks 'well the handler must know this is a dangerous dog coming towards us and I quite like these new people, so I must bark and be ferocious even more than normal to keep them safe' and every time the dog barks the new owner tries to reassure him, only dogs don't understand reassurance like that, so he only hears the new owner saying 'what a good boy you are to bark like that you had better carry on, here have a titbit'

2. Along comes a new owner and takes the dog home. The dog barks at another dog in the park; the owner thinks well there're no small children around to accidentally get knocked over, the other dog is a nice big placid labrador, and his owner doesn't look worried. My dog is on the lead so how about I just say 'you can go to the end of the lead, and rip its head off if you like, but I'm not joining in – it's up to you'. With a bit of luck your dog will think 'well hold on, if my new mum's not going to help me out with this then I had better shut up' you will (of course) have a titbit or two in your pocket, if you're lucky and you can reassure the other owner your dog is just making a lot of noise, then you can give the labrador a titbit, and your dog will probably demand his titbit. In fairness, he will start to think that other dogs turning up are actually something to be

looked forward to. Your dog has started to learn that there's actually a more rewarding behaviour than just barking first and asking questions later.

Now I don't want to be size-ist here and suggest that it's mostly little dogs that do this, but (like little people) they do seem to have a lot to say for themselves. Possibly if you've got control of a ten week old puppy that's going to grow into something enormous people take more trouble to sort out the problems when they begin.

It's very easy to say relax and calm down, but remember that dogs do not usually get into a fight, serious or otherwise. If a dog pitched into a fight at every opportunity it would not survive for long. If you are worried then find someone with a suitable other dog to pretend to be a stranger and 'meet' them in the park and see what happens – other dogs have to be preferably bigger and older and placid and more importantly have to have a handler who is not going to panic when your dog barks.

Make sure that your dog recognises that you are not going to back him up if he gets in fight, even if it is only a shouting match, he has to know he is on his own. If he does start barking then make sure if possible it is not rewarded by the dog getting what he wants, this means that the other dog goes away - preferably quickly. Make sure that he knows that if he walks past another dog without barking then you are going to be very pleased and reward him in some way, unfortunately he's learned one behaviour, now he has to learn a better one.

BUT REMEMBER - I, and I am sure you, won't like every person that you meet, you cannot expect your dog to like every dog it meets. It is enough that he walks past them in a civilised manner - do not try to force him into a friendship that isn't going to happen.

32. HIS TIME - YOUR TIME - THIS PLACE - THAT PLACE

I took a phone call from someone who was interested in bringing her puppy to training, now I must have been in the mood to chat because we talked about dogs and it turned out that she had an older (two and a half years) springer spaniel. She was happy about this dog because it was well socialised and did everything that it was told when it was in the hall where they trained, but it turned out that it wouldn't do anything when it was out because she had effectively taught this dog that at training it had to behave, but out on walks this was 'his time' and he could do what it wanted! So it did. It came when it wanted; socialised with whomever it wanted; hunted rabbits and pheasants whenever and wherever it wanted. So I asked her the question 'is it fun to own a dog like this?', and she said it certainly was at training, but then she admitted that she hated taking him for walks unless she kept him on the lead.

The moral of the story is that whatever we do at training only teaches the dog to do that particular thing at training. Sits have to be repeated at home, in the garden, on walks, when the dog wants to sit, when the dog doesn't want to sit, in fact everywhere until the dog learns that it means sit wherever he was when you gave him the order. It's the same with recall, retrieve, etcetera, etcetera, etcetera. By teaching him that a certain time is 'his time' and he doesn't have to behave means that the dog actually learns that he is more important than you and it's up to him whether he behaves or not and you cannot be surprised when the dog decides he doesn't want to behave at training anymore.

It is not up to the dog – it is up to you to be the boss every time and all the time. You have to be consistent, a recall means come here now, not when his time is finished, and a good recall may well be rewarded by the dog being allowed to go off again to play, but a bad recall can be 'punished' by further training until the dog decides it is more rewarding to behave properly.

33. PERMISSION TO MISBEHAVE

You are probably thinking what a stupid thing to say, no one gives their dog permission to misbehave. Oh yes they do! Just reflect a moment, the dog is supposed to be doing something like walking at heel, then it shoots off to talk to another dog. The owner stands there and laughs in an embarrassed fashion, then calls the dog back (which it ignores because it is having more fun talking to the other dog) and then calls it again. Eventually goes to fetch it and, funnily enough, the dog evades the owner and carries on with what it's doing. So eventually order is restored – and the dog has just had about two minutes of really rewarding behaviour misbehaving, so the exercise is repeated, and not surprisingly **the dog does exactly the same thing again** because he's just learnt that misbehaving is actually more fun.

So let's start again. The dog is walking to heel and it sees another dog it would like to talk to and thinks it might just go off, but the owner waves a titbit in front of his eyes and suddenly it's a better idea to stay with owner after all because she's got a really tasty titbit.

Alright, you weren't quick enough waving the titbit and he's gone, but you move like greased lightning and just after he's arrived at the other dog you are behind him and grab hold of his collar and pull him away from the other dog. You're cross that your dog is where he shouldn't be, net result is your dog had about five seconds of worthwhile behaviour and then got told off. The other people watching thought you looked silly sprinting across the room but **WHO CARES** and secretly they were quite impressed that you were making the effort to not let your dog benefit from misbehaving.

So you go back to the exercise and funnily enough handler stops being cross when the dog is walking at heel. It suddenly turns into a nice place to be and handler shows the dog again that handler's got a really tasty titbit and dog's walking to heel then he sees the other dogs that he would really like to go and talk to, but last time he didn't get far and it didn't last long, and handler waves that titbit under his nose, so perhaps the dog makes the choice of staying with handler with the titbit. **SUCCESS!**

There are times when good dog training is going to make you look rather stupid, you will have to put on a stupid high pitched 'girly' voice – but it will please your dog and make him wag his tail, you will have to call your dog and possibly jump up and down and look a fool to make your dog interested enough to come and see what you're doing – pretty stupid behaviour. But consider, the handler that is willing to do 'silly' things may well end up with a dog that is a pleasure to own. The handler that maintains his dignity at all times may end up with a dog that is a pain in the neck, out of the two I know which one is going to look most stupid.

34. I WOULDN'T LIKE TO MEET HIM ON A DARK NIGHT!

Well, you will meet him some day, probably not on a dark night more likely in the day time and because he's got a dog with him then you are going to wonder just how your dog is going to react.

If you're lucky and if you've brought your dog up well, then he'll be sociable and well trained, but you might have brought him up to act like a whirling dervish and to bark like mad – it's easy to do. You've seen them walking down the street and a dog comes towards them, they're a bit worried about the dog and they get him on a very short lead, when he starts barking they shout at him to be quiet.

Look at it from the dog's point of view, he's going quietly down the street and a dog walks towards him, his owner starts to get anxious, and he can just feel the vibes coming down the lead, so is this a vicious animal coming towards him? It must be I suppose, because why else would the owner be so nervous? Suddenly the owner is helping the dog to look big; owner's pulling him up on a short lead and dog starts to shout (bark) in order to keep the other (vicious) dog away. His owner starts to help as he's started barking (shouting) as well and they all speed up to get away quick from the vicious animal.

What you've got to remember is that there are three possible ways the dog can react, he can freeze and hope the other dog doesn't notice him. Well that's difficult for him to do because he's attached to you by a lead, or he can run away, again no he can't – he's attached to you by a lead, or he can talk to the dog – now if you panic and get him on a short lead and let yourself get tense now, that tension transfers to the dog whether or not you intend it to and that short lead makes your dog show himself off to his full height.   So, you are making your dog adopt an aggressive posture and if you try to reassure him like you would a small child then he perceives that you are praising him for being scared and logically if you are praising him for being scared then there must be something to be scared about. If he woofs and you tell him to shut up then perhaps he will perceive this as you showing a united defence with him and two individuals together are a lot braver than one.

And suddenly walking the dog is a lot less fun.

Now assuming your dog isn't really vicious – and bearing in mind that if he's been beaten up recently by a black labrador (example only - I've nothing against black labradors) then he might well think that all large black dogs are a bit iffy. When perhaps you find a dog walking towards you - first watch the owner, if he suddenly panics and grabs his dog then maybe he knows a lot more about his dog than you do. But if he's not bothered then don't panic about your dog, tell your dog it's up to him, he can sniff nicely, say hello, and walk on past, or he can act like a hooligan and start a fight, but it's up to him, you're not going to help! A lot of dogs, when they suddenly realise they're on their own suddenly decide they are not so brave after all.

35. FUN AND GAMES

If you've got a puppy then remember that your puppy is bred for playing with his litter mates, and his bites and nips will mean nothing to his brothers and sisters because they're wearing nice thick hairy coats to protect them – they will flipping well hurt you though! So don't take it personally, puppy doesn't hate you, he just doesn't know any better.

Don't grit your teeth, smile bravely and carry on playing when he bites you. That way puppy doesn't learn anything. If he doesn't play nicely then stop the game. Puppy will soon learn that biting means the end of the game, he likes the game, and he doesn't want it to end! So if he bites then 'scream in agony' and pretend it really hurts and end the game and the playtime -he will soon learn.

36. HAIRY TOES

I'm not talking about your hairy toes; I've no wish to know! Although I seem to remember hairy toes is a sign of a werewolf, I'm talking about your dog. Now when it's a puppy it won't have lived long enough to grow a lot of hair between its toes, but unless it's a short haired breed it will probably happen in time. What you should be aware of is that grass seeds may get trapped in amongst the excess hair and the seed will possibly work its way upwards into the dog's actual foot. It can go further and exit at the back of the leg. As you can imagine this will end up with a big fee at the vets, but what is even worse it will mean that you have a lame dog.

Simplest prevention is trimming the hair periodically. What is nicest/easiest is training the dog to accept you picking up the foot and handling it regularly. I do this when he's lying down having a cuddle, he may be a bit ticklish at first but they usually get used to it, especially if you start doing this before you either need to trim the hair, or what is more crucial, before the dog has something stuck between its toes and the whole area hurts like mad.

Start gradually, of course, just pick up the foot, put it down and give the dog a reward, next day pick up the foot and look at it and the day after feel between the toes. The dog won't care because he's going to get a reward at the end of it. When the dog is well used to it you can fiddle about down there with the scissors.

Although I mention this for the summer time, in the winter trimming his feet will have the advantage that he will trample less mud on your carpets, if you have to dry his feet there will be less hair there anyway and if he goes out in the snow he will not gather snowballs on his feet!

37. ISSUES

Now there are a few things you've got to remember – the dog is a dog, he is not a little human in a hairy coat. If he is a rescue dog he won't remember what a terrible life he's had as a start, you will be tempted to be nice to him, to spoil him, to let him jump up, jump on the sofa, chew things up – the dog will not understand that you are letting him do this to make up for his terrible beginning, he just thinks that this is the way that you are happy for him to behave. Start as you mean to go on.

Next thing is that usually dogs that are well brought up do not often need to be re-homed – dogs that need re-homing usually have 'issues'. Now some issues you can live with and some you can't, you have to change their thinking about what is the best way to behave in a situation.

For example – an issue may be that your dog is scared of men. I accept that he may have good reason to be scared of men, but that is in the past. If he now barks at men he is probably doing it to tell the men that they had better not come near me because 'I am a big fierce dog'. This is anti-social behaviour; you can't expect men to be happy to be barked at all the time.

What you may be tempted to do is to reassure him in the way that is most obvious to you. You stroke him and tell him in a nice voice 'don't do that Fido that's not nice'. Look at it from the dog's point of view – he's started barking and then you start stroking him and saying in a nice voice 'blah blah blah' (remember he doesn't understand English). He thinks you're praising him for barking – it's no wonder he carries on. Or perhaps rather than using the nice voice, you use a loud voice.

Look at this from the dog's point of view, he starts barking and you start shouting, are you joining in? So you've got to find a way of altering the dog's mind. First thing is to let him know that you don't like this behaviour – if he doesn't even know this much then there is no chance he will change.

Keep your hands off him. The chances are that he likes it when you touch him so remember when you touch him you are actually praising him. Don't shorten the lead when you see a chap coming. If you do then you tell the dog that something is about to happen and he needs to be alert. If you pull him back you can actually lift his front legs off the floor and this makes him look bigger and fiercer so you are helping him be aggressive.

There are two ways to go here. Firstly the chap may be a 'stooge' known to you and primed as to the way to react. If he is, then he can take a tasty treat out of his pocket and just drop it on the floor in front of the dog and keep walking. He doesn't stop, doesn't attempt to talk to you or the dog, just ignores the dog, but drops the treat letting the dog see and letting it eat the treat.

Now progress will be pretty quick. Your dog will decide that it is actually quite nice meeting men and it's not a good idea to bark at them to go away because he doesn't want them to go away he wants them to give him a treat. When the dog is happy to accept a treat then it's alright for the bloke to give him the treat by hand, but don't try and force it, you can only work as fast as the dog wants to go.

If you haven't got any trained 'stooges' to hand, then you can achieve the same results by producing the treat yourself, get the dog's attention on the treat before the bloke is close enough and before the dog starts barking and give the dog the treat. Hopefully the dog will learn that it's good when men appears because it means that Mum/Dad gives him treats, eventually you can give him the treat as a reward for not barking.

Remember that treats don't have to mean titbits, toys work just as well.

If the dog doesn't like men or visitors to the house then you can have a pot of titbits by the door, give the visitor one and tell him to drop it on the floor in front of the dog, but tell him not to talk to the dog, don't look him in the eye (in dog language this behaviour is very challenging) just to ignore him until the dog is ready to come to him. You have to make the dog think that visitors are great because titbits happen, visitors are not scary because it's up to the dog to investigate them and they are not going to force attention on to the dog until he is ready for it.

If you can't make your visitors behave by your rules, then either don't invite them, or put the dog away so he doesn't meet them.

One thing you have to be aware of is that it is very flattering if your dog thinks you are a really terrific person but he thinks that everyone else in world is horrible. You are in a dilemma here because it's great fun and the temptation is to allow this behaviour to carry on, but one day you'll have to take him to the vets, or board him at a kennels, or get a friend to look after him for an afternoon and this behaviour will suddenly be not so much fun.

38. ALGAL BLOOMS

This sounds totally boring and irrelevant, but believe me, you should know about them. In any body of water there is a totally natural algae which is normally no problem. But on days that are hot and sunny, particularly if you have several days the same and the water is not moving, it may 'bloom', that is reproduce when it produces a powerful toxin which can **KILL** your dog if it swims in it or drinks some of it.

Some of these blooms look like foam, scum, or mats on the surface, they can be blue, bright green, brown or red, but some blooms may not look any different to 'normal' water, the water may or may not smell, and, to cap it all, not all algal blooms are toxic anyway.

When an algal bloom is toxic it can kill or seriously sicken an animal in 15 or 20 minutes. If you think your dog has been in contact with a toxic bloom then get it to a vet pronto, if you take it home and watch it until there are definite symptoms then it may be too late to save the animal. If clean water is available then wash off the 'toxic' water, but **do not delay**.

You may be wondering how often this happens. I have never had a dog die or been affected by it, but I have spoken to people who have lost dogs from it. I have seen notices on stretches of water warning of the possibility of it and my dog that likes swimming goes on the lead immediately – it is just not something that you can take chances with. In a traditional wet 'British' summer it's not a problem, but it may be more of a problem in the future with global warning.

39. TIMING

They say that the secret to good comedy is timing, and it's also true in dog training. Just suppose for a moment that your problem with your dog is that he always barks terribly at other dogs in the street. You walk down the road and you can see someone coming with a dog, your dog sees it as well and he starts to become alert, you go nearer –now he's very alert and you get opposite the dog. Your dog is barking like mad and you are telling him to shut up and be quiet, only you now have to shout to make yourself heard over the racket he's making. Only by this stage he's so wound up he's not listening to you – it's so embarrassing, he's now making death threats to the other dog.

Okay let's do it another way, you're walking down the same street and you see the same dog coming towards you – and your dog sees it as well and starts to get alert. You tell him 'no, you don't like him getting wound up' and with a bit of luck he'll say okay and calm down again - because you got the correction in quickly! And it was at a time when he was mildly out of his normal nice calm state so he found it easy to obey. Plus you are learning that other dogs passing are not a big problem, so you no longer get tense when other dogs appear, and because your dog recognises that you get tense when other dogs appear he starts to think that other dogs are a big problem so he gets worse, so you get more tense, and so forth, and you end up walking your dog at two o'clock in the morning when the only people you meet are burglars and other people who don't know how to change their dogs' behaviour.

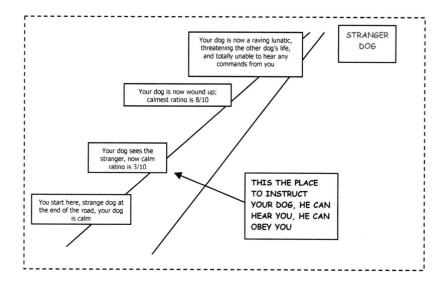

Your dog is now a raving lunatic, threatening the other dog's life, and totally unable to hear any commands from you

STRANGER DOG

Your dog is now wound up; calmest rating is 8/10

Your dog sees the stranger, now calm rating is 3/10

You start here, strange dog at the end of the road, your dog is calm

THIS THE PLACE TO INSTRUCT YOUR DOG, HE CAN HEAR YOU, HE CAN OBEY YOU

40. TRAINING FOR THE DOG?

I don't think we would get many takers if we advertised dog training as 'human training' instead. But that is the honest truth of the matter – people may recognise that their 'new addition' needs to go to training - but in actual fact, it is often the handler that needs to learn the 'right' way to approach things. Nowadays people take on pets never having lived with an animal before, they have no concept of seeing things from the dog's point of view, and they actually have no inherent belief that this is a dog and not a little human in a shaggy coat. That is the most useful thing that we can bring out in a person – the ability to look at things from the dogs point of view, to see what they are seeing, to think what they are thinking.

When you are doing anything with a dog you have to bear in mind 'What you are teaching the dog isn't necessarily what the dog is learning'. Which is a bit of a b***** really, life would be so much easier if that wasn't true, but it also makes life so much more interesting as well, and so much more rewarding when your dog does something that is exactly what you want, but something that you didn't believe that he could do.

Am I talking rubbish, probably, but let me give you an example. I have two female dogs, an old one, Ticket and a young one, Kipper, both black working Cocker spaniels. Ticket is probably ready for her bus pass and while I love her dearly I tend to do more with the young one. I wanted to see if the young dog could pull off my sock if I attached a tuggy toy to it for her to pull, I've never previously asked her to pull, I set it up and to be honest she was being a bit thick and didn't understand. All of a sudden Ticket, who had never done this before, got off her bed, gave the young one a condescending look, took hold of the tug and pulled the sock off my foot perfectly!   Ticket again showed the wisdom of age over youth a couple of weeks later, I wanted to see if the Kipper could pick up my keys, they do have a plastic strap on them so it wasn't as hard as it sounds, I threw the keys out on the lawn, Kipper bounced around and sniffed but wouldn't pick them up. Old dog gets up, throws Kipper a withering look, picks the keys up and brings them back perfectly.   She had never done this before, young dog copied her and the next time picked up the keys.

41. SCOOP THE POOP

Well you've got to haven't you, unless you are lucky enough to be miles from anywhere in a place where no one else is remotely likely to step in what your dog leaves behind. If you haven't already discovered them try buying 'nappy bags', bags made for the disposal of used nappies, they don't have ventilation holes and they sit in your pocket and don't take up a lot of room. It is tempting to re-use bags from the shops, the first time you discover (too late) that the bag has a hole in it you will decide this is not a good plan.

A question that bothers me occasionally is that you can carry a good supply of bags for years and years, the first time you go out without a bag your dog will immediately decide it needs to go despite the fact that it went half an hour ago - dogs and kids always let you down!

One thing I should add is that if you have a very large dog that produces 'piles' of a very large size, the nappy bags may not be large enough, hard luck – that's why I go for smaller sized dogs.

There are many things that irritate me; principal amongst them is why are there more calories in any food that tastes good? But, apart from that, I really get wound up by people who pick up their dog's poop AND THEN HANG THE PLASTIC BAG ON THE NEAREST TREE SO THAT EVERYONE HAS TO LOOK AT IT. This is really, really stupid behaviour. I don't want to look at your dog's mess, I'm really pleased you picked it up but you have got to go the whole way and put it in an appropriate bin. Plastic bags do not magically move themselves when no one is watching, they hang there being conspicuous, until eventually they fall off and get wet and muddy and if you are lucky some poor unfortunate eventually comes along and takes them away.

Having said that, and I speak from bitter experience here, if you scoop the poop routinely but then put it in a pocket until you get to the bin, don't forget it. Don't do as I have done and got home and hung up your coat with the full bag in the pocket and, through circumstance, don't wear the coat for a while, then it all gets a little whiffy, and if you can't find the source of the smell it will get a lot whiffy. This is not a good plan, even if you love your dog it does not do your reputation for housework a lot of good!

42. RAMPS AND CARS

Now I hope that your dog is capable of jumping in the car, but just consider what he will be like in ten years time – if he is getting arthritic it might not be so easy, don't forget you are going to be 10 years older as well, how easy will it be for you to lift him in the car? If you've got a small/medium sized dog then no problem, but if he's large and you may want him to walk up a ramp into your car in the future then just consider teaching him to do this now. When he gets older and a little bit shaky he might not be so willing to walk on a ramp if it's a bit scary and he's never done it in this life before.

This is true – would I lie to you? I looked after Sam, a large heavy labrador who was fast approaching old age. Ticket, my old spaniel had quite early decided it was too much effort to jump in the car, and she was quite happy to be lifted and helped. Sam increasingly found it was difficult. I didn't like lifting him because he was big and heavy and his owner had already damaged his own back lifting Sam out of the bath. Sam was a boy and he didn't like my hands going anywhere near his delicate bits., Every time we went for a walk he managed to dive in the canal so I was usually having to lift him when he was wet and muddy. I eventually got him a ramp and taught him to go up it quite happily, but of course while it was up I also expected Ticket to use it. She was perfectly happy about going up while I was teaching Sam his party trick, but when Sam was happy about going up my old spaniel started trying to go to one side and saying she would rather be lifted. Eventually I worked out what was wrong. She actually preferred being lifted, because that way she sort of got a cuddle as well and usually a quick word that she was special, she would go up the ramp if there were biscuits around, but otherwise she'd much rather have a lift. I had to be hard, and soon we reached an agreement, once she was in the car I gave her a quick cuddle and a kind word.

43. HE EATS WHAT!

I hope you're not eating tea. I really wish that I didn't know about dogs that eat disgusting things, but unfortunately I do. Sam eats dog pooh! Isn't that disgusting! An in-joke amongst the people that know him is that he would never bite a burglar, but if he gives them a lick then they'd better go straight to hospital. I don't know why he does it, except that obviously to him it tastes nice. I refuse to experiment further than that. He doesn't like all dogs' pooh, he doesn't eat his own or my dogs' pooh that is sometimes in the garden. But sometimes when we're out

95

he can actually smell and seek out a particularly delicious pile. I think it has something to do with what the dogs are fed with, and possibly the fact that their bodies are not absorbing all the nutrients from the food. He knows not to do it in front of me and when we are on a walk I always make sure he is in front of me where I can see him. I have to let him be a dog and sniff other dog's pooh, that's normal dog behaviour, but now, when he takes a bite, I can growl at him and he'll drop what he's got and move on.

Half of me says 'He's a dog, this is what dogs do, stop asking him to be a human, and the other dogs don't find it disgusting' and that argument is logically correct, but still - it's pretty horrible. I could walk him in a muzzle but it doesn't bother me enough for that, and strangely it never seems to upset his stomach. He never seems tempted to eat horse pooh, which my own dogs find irresistible, but because horses are vegetarian that doesn't seem so disgusting.

I did hear of a dog that obsessively eats slugs - and later vomits them back on the carpet, so really eating dog pooh isn't so bad after all. I suppose that dog owner had a glorious garden which never suffered slug damage. Incidentally, if your dog does eat snails, along with slugs they carry the larval stage for Heartworm. At the moment Britain can be smug because it doesn't have much Heartworm, but with global warming and dogs travelling abroad it is something that we are probably going to have to cope with in the future.

44. REACHING THE POTENTIAL

I listened to a talk once from someone who was big in training dogs as assistance dogs for the disabled. She related a tale of how they had trained a dog and homed it with a lady who used a wheelchair. This lady happened to live by the sea and it must have been autumn because when she took the dog for a walk in the late afternoon there was no one on the beach, then the electric wheelchair broke down! The lady lived alone so she knew that there was nobody to worry about her getting home and what was worse was that she didn't have her mobile phone with her. Out of desperation she tried sending her assistance dog to fetch her mobile phone, he was used to doing this in the house but she had never tried it out of doors, so this really was an act of desperation, the lady must have breathed a sigh of relief when the dog disappeared in the direction of the house.

But what the disabled lady didn't know was that after they had left the house her carer had arrived, the carer wasn't worried that the lady was out with the dog because that was normal, so she turned down the bed – and put the mobile phone under the pillow on her bed which was where it was handy if the lady had to call for help in the night then she left!

So the dog got back to the house, couldn't find the mobile phone where it was usually to be found and where he expected it to be, but found it under the pillow. <u>He had never before looked for it there</u>. Then he galloped back to the beach to take the phone to his owner who was then able to phone for help and avoid hypothermia.

You might be thinking, 'what a wonderful dog' that's what I thought, but what you shouldn't be thinking is 'I wish I had that sort of dog' because the important thing to remember is that it possibly was once an ordinary 'mutt', but it had been trained to think for itself, to work out solutions to problems without being told the answers. Dogs are trained as Police dogs, shepherd dogs, assistance dogs for the deaf, rescue dogs, sniffer dogs for drugs; guns; explosives; money; cancer; bodies; fire accelerants; bees and probably a lot more things that I have forgotten and probably some things in the future yet to be thought of – the possibilities are endless.

My own dogs are good at picking things up and fetching. I have taught Kipper, to fetch the empty dog dishes when I'm doing the washing up. Both Kipper and Ticket, the older dog, fetch my shoes or slippers when asked. They are sort of assistance dogs – not because I'm disabled but because I'm lazy and besides they enjoy it.

I actually know someone whose partner has a habit of going to the toilet and then shouting at her to please bring him a new toilet roll, so she has trained the dog to take a new toilet roll to her very grateful partner! The possibilities are endless.

It is possible to 'teach an old dog new tricks' if you go about it the right way. There is more to life than sit, heel and come. There are admittedly limitations with your dog's size and what it has been genetically programmed to learn, but apart from that the only limitation is how far you want to take it, and how many things you can think of to teach it!

45. INSURANCE

My first dog was healthy for a number of years and I didn't have veterinary insurance, and I must admit I felt rather smug. She then had a bad back, which turned out to be a very serious condition which could have led to an operation on her spine. I didn't opt for the operation as they couldn't guarantee success and luckily the problem was managed by acupuncture, which had to be on a regular basis and cost me a fortune, it was then discovered that she had a very rare and untreatable tumour and I eventually had to make the decision that I wouldn't put her through any more and she was put to sleep. It was expensive (very) and my next dog was insured.

She was healthy and ten years later I very nearly cancelled the insurance, it was only apathy that meant I didn't get around to it. She then got ill, I'm not saying I've got all my money back yet but boy, am I glad she's insured, don't misunderstand me, she would have got the veterinary treatment anyway, even if I had to take out bank loans and sell my house, but it has made me appreciate the insurance.

Kipper has only third party insurance and I've decided I'm going to up this to veterinary insurance the next time I renew the policy. I think you are very foolish if you don't at least have third party insurance. Your dog could cause a car crash which could cause injuries which could lead to you being sued for basically everything you've got. There are not many companies that offer third party only, but if you look hard enough you'll find one.

I will not tell anyone they ought to have veterinary insurance. It's a crystal ball job to know the future and I don't know if you'll claim on it or not, but if you don't then you and your dog have been lucky. But just consider what the vets are able to do these days and veterinary bills can be eye watering – it's worth considering insurance and if you don't go for it then at least put an equivalent sum of money in a special account. If it's still there when you lose the dog you can go out and spend it on the next dog.

46. THEFT AND RANSOM

Dogs are worth stealing, not only for resale, dog fighting and pelts, they are worth kidnapping to get a ransom from their owners, which is a terrible crime because, let's face it, how many of us would not be willing to pay to get our dogs back? But for all the dogs that are stolen and end up in new homes, a considerable amount get dumped or lost and end up in pet shelters. Now you may think that pet wardens are able to accurately describe a stray animal, but that simply isn't true and while you might be frantically looking for your pet you might be ignoring something described as what he isn't. Think about having your pet micro-chipped at the very least and hope that if he ever does end up in a rescue centre they run a scanner over him. Or consider having his ear tattooed, which could be a more worthwhile thing because it means that even those people who don't own a scanner will be able to do something about tracing his real home. I had Kipper tattooed, yes it obviously hurt at the time, but two minutes later she had forgotten it.

Unbelievable fact, while it is the job of local councils to pick up the bodies of dogs killed on the roads there is nothing to say that they have to scan the bodies for micro-chips they can simply destroy the bodies, meaning that you may never know what has happened to a missing dog. There is a campaign to change this.

47. I'D JUST LIKE TO POINT THIS OUT

It's a natural human behaviour that if you want something from another 'person' and they need some extra information you might well point to the item you want. That's super, but remember - **DOGS DON'T DO THIS.** It's perfectly possible to teach your dog all about pointing, but if your dog doesn't understand that when you point it's supposed to look at where your finger is pointed to, it will probably look at the end of your finger.

If you're up for teaching your dog about pointing then start by throwing a toy or something a short distance away, crouch down by his head, point at the object so your dog is looking along your arm at the toy and then send him to fetch, when that's achieved throw the toy, or a treat, and **don't let him see where it's gone**, and then crouch down and point your arm and his head in the direction it's gone. Unless he's stupid he will soon work out that by going where you are pointing, he will find something nice. An added thing to remember is the wind direction - the wind is going to carry the scent of the object, if you're sensible you set things up so that the dog has to go upwind, along the scent trail coming from the object.

This should work and a bit of repetition will mean that the dog gets used to listening to you for helpful information. Gradually you will find that just by pointing in the appropriate direction, even if you're not lined up by his head, he will look in the right area – your dog is learning to understand your pointing. One other thing, sometimes it is useful for your dog to see something that is helpful for him to know, if you say to your dog 'WATCH' and you look at the thing you want him to see rather than looking at your dog, he will learn to look in the same direction. He is learning that you are helping him. Once he knows this, it is more likely that he will listen to you when you tell him things – life gets easier.

48. RELEASE WORDS

When you are training with your dog and he's walking nicely to heel (for example), then there will come a time when you are satisfied that he's done enough and can go and play. Some people make the mistake of telling the dog 'good boy, go and play' in all innocence this is all right, but there will come a time when you are teaching him something else or something new, and perhaps say 'good boy' to tell him that what he is doing is right and then the dog will quite rightly think that you have just told him he has finished and he can go and play. This can either cause chaos to your training, or can cause a disaster to happen when there is a truck passing on the road. Get in the habit of telling him, for example, 'finished – go play' that way confusion will not happen.

49. SWALLOW THIS

Unless you are incredibly lucky your dog will have to take a pill sometime in his life, at the moment my dog is taking four, twice a day. Now there are a few very greedy dogs who will take a pill because it is offered to them, and there are a few clever people who can pop a pill down a dog's throat before the dog has realised what is going on. But for the rest of us who are struggling may I suggest subterfuge? Just buy a tin of Dog Food the original, not the fancy sort, it comes out as a sort of jelly with 'meaty mush' bits in it, scoop out a lump with a spoon and push the pill into the middle – if your dog is anything like mine he will just be so pleased to be given something so tasty he'll swallow it before he notices the pill. In actual fact, because I have three dogs, she will eat it even faster in case the other one gets it.

50. AGAIN ON THE SUBJECT OF CARS

Now, of course, you are a responsible citizen and you have taught your dog to travel settled and quiet, have you ever considered what would happen if you crashed? Your other passengers are wearing their seat belts and they will be securely fastened in, but your dog, if he's unsecured, will fly around the car at a great rate of knots. I'm not talking about the fact that he will die in the impact, that is terrible enough, but there's another fact that you ought to consider, if he comes flying over the back of your seat and into you then you may well end up in a wheelchair and not looking for another dog but thinking about an assistance dog instead. I'm not trying to interfere, it's up to you and I won't be travelling in your car anyway, but if you are sensible you will travel your dog either behind a dog guard, or in a dog crate, or wearing an appropriate dog seat belt – just in case.

Another thing to think about is that if your dog is quite happy sitting in a seat and never moves if you have a car that has air bags that go off in a collision, then your dog will suddenly get an air bag in his face. Will it do him more damage than the accident? I don't know, but again it's worth thinking about.

51. IT REALLY IS YOUR DOG AND YOU DO KNOW BEST

You know more about your dog than I do, I will give you suggestions but if you do not think they make sense do not act on them. If you disagree with what I say you are quite at liberty to challenge it, I will give you my reasons and we'll talk about it, but if I tell you something and it totally screws up your dog then although I admit it will make me unhappy I will still go home without your dog whilst you are stuck with him. When you own a dog you will meet lots of people who will rush to give you 'good' advice, maybe it's something really clever that worked for their dog, or something that their Dad used to do with the family pet, or just their own warped idea, I suggest you smile sweetly and then say 'What an interesting idea, I'll bear that in mind/cross the road if I see you coming/phone the RSPCA/talk to someone who actually owns a dog or two and see if they think it's a good idea' but basically go away and think about it, and if it still seems like a good idea, and if this person does actually know what they're on about, then maybe you could consider trying it.

A work of caution, beware the owner who has one very well trained dog and sets themselves up as the local expert, one very well trained dog does not make them wise in the ways of dogs. Ticket, the second dog that I owned was very steady, almost to the point of wondering whether she was still awake (no, that's not true), but I certainly did take her

104

to the vets and ask if there was a medical reason for this. Of course she was well-behaved; she didn't have enough energy to be naughty. I have since discovered that she actually has a thyroid problem and it isn't down to my 'brilliant' training after all. And with hindsight, she had the thyroid problem for a long time, but the vet had not bothered to check for that and they thought that she was overweight because I fed her too much, I wish I had insisted earlier, but you just presume that your vet knows more than you do (I no longer presume this).

52. TREATS OR BRIBERY AND CORRUPTION

I like treats and incidentally I also give treats to my dogs. I go to work to earn wages and if I didn't get wages then I wouldn't go. Some people work on the principle that you should never give your dogs a treat and they should do things because they love you – yeah get real! But you have to remember that while your dog is happy working for a simple treat such as a boring dog biscuit when there is nothing better to do, when there is something exciting happening then he's not going to be interested in your boring old dog biscuit. If he's not interested in your treats then try adding something interesting like chopped up cold cooked sausage, give him a good sized chunk initially - let him know what's on offer, after that you can choose whether he's rewarded by a biscuit or a piece of sausage.

If he's not turned on by sausage try a piece of cooked meat, you can buy cooked meat ready sliced and it's very easy, or a taste of cheese, or frankfurter, or a cat treat, or use whatever comes to hand. Incidentally if he's not turned on by cold meat try zapping it in a microwave and get it nice and warm and smelly. Experiment - to be truthful the right thing to use is whatever works. You might not even use food; toys can be magnetic to some dogs, especially squeaky toys. If you are expecting him to be excited by a toy then make sure that you keep control of the toy, put it away where he can't get it and make it very exciting when it does come out.

In club at the moment we have a largish hairy terrier type called Teasel who was a rescue. I always thought she was bright that was never the problem, but she wasn't that keen on doing work - even for a food treat, then her mother borrowed a squeaky toy from another handler, and Teasel came alive, oh yes, she would fetch, she would stay (impossible before) she would do anything if it meant she was rewarded with her squeaky toy. She did actually rip her mother's coat to get at her squeaky toy once, when her mother was silly enough to leave it unattended.

If you are using a food treat to teach something like walking to heel off the lead then remember the dog has to be aware that the treat is there, wave it under his nose if necessary before you start, and when you set off walking remember that the dog has to believe that it's possible that he will get the treat. If you hold the treat in a position in front of your left leg and your dog sniffs the floor or something then again wave the treat in front of him, get his attention back on the treat, and then gradually put the treat back into position as you start off walking again.

53. TEENAGE THUGS AND ASBOs

I'm not sure that anyone has ever given a dog an Asbo but it will probably happen soon and apparently it's a very trendy name in some parts of the country. What I really want to point out is that your dog will probably/certainly/possibly go through a phase when he literally does turn into a thug; hopefully he will grow out of it pretty quick - almost certainly before he gets his old age pension.

If you think about your dog if he lived in the wild in a pack he would be a nice little puppy being subservient to all the other dogs; then he would grow up a bit, probably to the point of being a teenager and he would be playing with the rest of his litter mates and it would look very physical and there would be a lot of growling and mouthing and physical wrestling, and then he would get a bit bigger, and he would get over confident and think he could take on his Dad, and his Dad would very soon beat him up, noisily but probably not seriously, and then your puppy would settle down and know his place in the pack.

But he doesn't live in a pack, he's only got you to play with, and you have to give him boundaries because you really don't want him biting and wrestling with you – okay well it might be fun when he's a baby but he's not going to understand why you no longer want to play with him when he's a big strong teenager. You have to always maintain the illusion that you're bigger stronger and smarter than he is if, just for example, he likes to chew the lead - well it's more fun than walking to heel, then let him chew all he likes - but buy a can of foul tasting chew, stop and spray that on the lead. If he gives up on the lead, but instead jumps up and bites your hand or your coat, well okay tell him that's okay but every time he does it he causes you to squirt him with the squeezy bottle of water you just happen to have in your hand. It's not you doing it, he's causing it to happen by jumping up and biting, but on the same principle, if he is walking nicely to heel and not jumping and not biting TELL HIM YOU LIKE THAT BEHAVIOUR, REWARD HIM, MAKE A FUSS OF HIM.

There are lots of ways that he can try it on, you just have to think about what he's doing and why, and you have to think about some devious horrible way that will make him work out that it probably isn't a good idea. While it's perfectly possible to train him not to do something because you tell him not to do it, it's a lot more worthwhile to let him decide for himself that something isn't a good idea or alternatively for him to work out that doing a certain thing is a good idea because that gets him something nice.

I don't want to really depress you if you've already got the 'wrong' type, but in my experience male dogs are more likely to have a phase where they turn into thugs, I could say it's because females have more sense but in reality males hopefully grow into being the leader of the pack and then they get lots of sex and children and that is the reason they were ultimately put on this planet. There are certain breeds that enjoy thuggish behaviour, I don't claim to know everything about all breeds but of the ones I know about boxers are possibly the worse, and I don't mean they are nasty but just that they enjoy being silly – if you own a boxer you have to have a sense of humour. Labradors can be spectacularly bouncy at times, so can lurchers/whippets, and I've known a Dalmatian that was either stupid or had a sense of humour and I could never work out which.

Another beware here, if your dog is being stupid then be careful about putting your hands on him to correct him, if he loves you then he will probably like you putting your hands on him, so effectively you are rewarding him for being stupid! Think about it.

54. TIP OF THE DAY

Confucius says that if you're putting your plastic bag package in a dog bin – don't breathe in!

55. FINISHED AT INFANTS, MOVING ON TO COMPREHENSIVE

Well, if you're still reading congratulations, hopefully it means that you've got a young dog that's growing up nicely. Just ask yourself a question – are you still acting like he's a little puppy, are you so indulgent that you tell him he's a 'good boy' every time he eventually sits, despite the fact that you had to ask him twenty three times and started to ask him about half an hour ago? Now is the time to grasp the nettle and accept that he knows what sit means, and if you ask him to 'sit' and he does so straight away then by all means tell him he's a good boy, and you could even give him a treat if it was a very nice sit. But don't indulge him forever. Ask him once, the second time tell him – and sound a bit strict, and if you have to tell him again then do it in a voice that sounds like if you have to tell him again then you might just pull his leg off! AND DON'T TELL HIM HE'S A GOOD BOY AFTERWARDS, he's only a good boy if he did it first time he was asked. He has to learn that actions have consequences, and ignoring Mum or Dad means no praise or titbits.

Having said that we should all recognise that there are times when he isn't going to sit - he is still a youngster and while he should sit if nothing exciting is going on, if there's something very interesting going on then it just isn't going to happen. In actual fact, if you ask him to sit and he doesn't because his mind is elsewhere then should you have asked him to sit in the first place? Have you just given him a lesson in ignoring instructions? Think about it. Every time you give your dog an instruction you should be willing to place a bet that he is going to follow the instruction, if he doesn't then send the money to me.

56. WHEN ONE ALONE IS NOT ENOUGH

There may well come a time when it's not enough to only have one dog, and let's face it you are already taking the time to walk one dog and run your life round one dog, so having a second dog isn't that big a jump. So a puppy turns up, and fits in quite nicely with the old dog, which you love dearly and vow that he will always be your number one. Puppy recognises that old dog is the number one dog, after all he's far bigger than puppy anyway, but puppy grows up and starts to think well maybe he could beat up the old dog and be number one instead, so maybe he does, and old dog knows the score and recognises that this young thing is far more able than he is so he will now accept being number two. Only you see this happen, and you are full of righteous indignation that how dare this young fit adolescent beat up your dear old dog that you love dearly and that you are going to take pains to treat the old dog as number one, and that is where things start to go wrong.

Young dog is now confused over whether he is number one or number two, so he beats up the old dog again, old dog doesn't actually want to argue about it - he's quite happy being number two (that is how nature has organised things, so that the pack has the most able leader which means that the species will survive), again you get cross with young dog - who is after all only trying to do what is natural in dog language, so young dog works out that he'd better only beat the old dog up when you are out of sight. You now have a problem, you can't be with the dogs twenty four hours a day, and when you're not there things go wrong.

Let's go through it again, puppy joins the pack, things are happy, old one is number one. Puppy gets bigger, there comes a time when the dogs <u>between them</u> decide puppy is number one – old dog is number two, both dogs recognise this, you don't like it but you accept it and accept this is the way that <u>they</u> have decided it, and you now treat the young dog as number one. Life is happy and serene, and when the new number one goes out into the garden first (as is his right) you then make a big fuss of the old one. And they all live happily ever after.

57. CLICKER TRAINING

You've probably heard of clicker training along the way, so let's talk about it. A clicker is a little gadget that you can put your finger on and make a 'click' sound. This sound is used to mark a behaviour that you like. Now a lot of the time training goes wonderfully by conventional means with the dog quite willing to do what you want it to do, but sometimes the dog doesn't want to co-operate or doesn't understand and you need another tool to get over the problem. This is the sort of thing that is perfect for clicker training.

What you've got to accept is that you <u>cannot</u> instantly cure the whole problem at once. If your dog doesn't, for instance, pick up things in his mouth then you can't teach him to do a perfect retrieve in one go. You've got to break everything down into very small stages, and every time that he does the behaviour that you like, you've got to click a clicker and follow it up with a reward, and the reward has to be worthwhile to make the dog wants another, but small enough that it's swallowed in a second otherwise training is going to take years!

The good news is that this is the sort of training that can be done indoors in the warm, you don't want lots of distractions about, have your dog off the lead, and hopefully you've either got a naturally greedy dog or he hasn't just eaten his tea.

If your dog hasn't met the clicker before then just start of by dropping a handful of treats on the floor, your dog will hopefully hoover them all up, and every time he goes to pick one up you are going to click. So hopefully your dog will think 'I like this training', but from now he's got to earn his clicks. Now get the toy you want him to fetch and put it somewhere handy, your dog hopefully will think 'what's that' and turn his head towards it, and you will click, and follow it up with a reward, and the dog will think 'that was a very tasty treat, what can I do to make mum give me another' he probably won't know, but out of curiosity he will eventually turn and look at the toy again, and you will click and treat, that's stage one. When your dog has learnt that to make you give him a click he's only got to look at the toy then you can move on to the next stage – now you don't click your dog for just looking, and he will think 'oh b**** why has Mum stopped clicking I enjoyed that, what have I got to do to get a click out of Mum?' and with a bit of luck, and a bit of patience from you, he will move towards the toy – and you can click!. Now you reward your dog for moving towards the toy, and eventually for moving right up to the toy and putting his nose on it, and then when he gets frustrated because you've stopped clicking him for touching it with his nose, he will hopefully open his mouth and eventually put his mouth round the toy, and then only click and reward when he picks it up, and then click and reward when he takes a step towards you with it in his mouth, and you can imagine the rest.

Remember, the dog is in control of the treats, if he does something that you like then click it and YOU MUST GIVE HIM A TREAT AFTERWARDS, but make sure that the sound of the click happens at the same instant as the dog is doing the act that you like. I don't know how long this training is going to take, it all depends on the dog and how clever you are at making the 'clicks' at the right time, but make sure that he conquers one stage before going on to the next. When he knows one stage then move on gradually, make it easy for him to succeed. If it all goes wrong then go back to something he can do, let him succeed, give him a treat and finish the session of training, next day start again with something that he knows.

My dogs love clicker training, when they understand what is wanted they are very quick to offer lots of behaviours in order to find out the one that earns the click. You can teach lots of things with this, but in order to keep it simple only try to teach one thing at a time!

58. DON'T LIKE CARS

Some dogs don't like cars, which is strange and illogical to us but very sensible to a dog although they're not going to explain why. So, what you have to do is alter its perception of cars, once it starts to think that cars are marvellous and wonderful your life will be much easier. Assuming you've got a hatchback open up the boot, then go back into the house and put some really tasty smelly food in the dogs bowl, it helps if the dog is hungry, carry this dish out to the car in full view of the dog and hopefully dog will know it's his bowl and he'd really like to eat the contents, and then put it in the back of the car. If you're lucky the dog will be so convinced it's his supper he will leap in the car and start eating, if he's shy of doing this or he's too small to jump into the car then lift him in and then let him eat the food, and then let him get out. Lesson over. Next meal, or when he's hungry again, repeat, this time he'll be happier to get in, after all last time all that happened was that he got to eat the food! When the dog is happy to get in the car and eat the food, then try shutting the hatch down, and when he's happy try starting the car, and when he's happy try driving ten foot down the drive and back again, after all there's nothing to object to, only getting in the car and eating lovely food and possibly (when he's happy and ready) driving ten foot or more.

If he's not into food, or alternatively if he is into toys, keep a toy in the car, and let him jump in and find it and then have a marvellous game. A word of warning, although to start with you may have to let him see the toy before he's willing to jump in, after a time you'll be able to move the toy so it is out of sight until he is in the car, this way he'll not be able to say 'I'm not getting in the car unless my toy is there', because one day you'll not have his toy handy.

In summary – make it a nice experience, only go one step further when he's happy with the previous lesson. Make car trips have happy endings, what does it matter if you drive one hundred yards to the park if he learns that nice things result from getting in cars.

59. FEEDING TIME AT THE ZOO

There is a common misconception, I could call it an old wives' tale, that you should be able to make the dog sit and wait for its dinner until you tell it to eat, and that you should be able to take it's dinner away any time you want to. I don't agree, if you were responsible for feeding me and you made me sit and wait for my dinner or took it away when I was in the middle of eating it, then I would seriously get annoyed. I like my food!

Some of this is people worrying about the dog getting possessive about his food when there is a child around, and I agree to a point because if things do go wrong then ultimately it is the dog that is going to be punished or put to sleep. Let's change the subject slightly, if there are dogs and kids in the same household then **children should be taught that they are never to go near the feed bowl and they are never to touch the dog when he is in his bed.** The dog's bed should be somewhere that it can go to get away from the kids! Everyone should have a place to call their own - especially the dog.

If you have a dog that is very enthusiastic about his food then you might have difficulties getting the food down on the floor before the dog starts eating, this isn't on, the dog should at least wait until it's on the floor, if he does get 'over the top' when food is coming then put the food back on the work surface, make him realise that jumping up means the food takes longer to arrive, then try and put it down again, and hopefully you'll get further because the dog won't know if it's going on the floor or not, but if he jumps up at the bowl then back on the surface it goes, what you want the dog to realise that it's his thuggish behaviour that makes the food take longer to arrive. Don't get mad, don't command the dog to 'behave', if your dog gets worse instead of better than abandon the plan and think again.

You could always try plan B. This is also more appropriate for the dog that is aggressive about his food. Make his meal but split it between two dishes and put the most boring half of it in the first dish, feed him that and he'll finish very quickly because it was actually only half a meal, then give him the second. You need the dog to work out that it's a bit silly being aggressive to you because you have the ability to give him some more and furthermore you are now giving him the best part of his dinner. When you are happy that your dog is not going to bite your hand off, give him half the feed first and let him eat it, and then he'll look at you in hopeful expectation, and then, instead of giving him his second dish, take a bit from it and put it in his bowl, you can repeat this as often as you like or until the food is finished!

What we are trying to do is alter the dog's perception, instead of the natural instinctive behaviour to drive anyone else away from food that he needs to keep him alive, you are actually making him think that it's a really good idea to let people go to his dish because they possibly give him some really nice food.

A word of commiseration here to people who own hungry greedy Labradors, they seem to have the ability to devour huge meals in one gulp – mealtimes are not usually a problem, they are just over very quickly.

60. BLOW THE WHISTLE

You might like to consider using a whistle, I certainly do and would recommend it, but don't think it's a wonderful thing by itself, your dog can just as easily ignore you blowing a whistle as it can ignore you calling it. I use a gun dog whistle, which is a long thin one, it's got $210\frac{1}{2}$ stamped on the back, which probably means something to those that know, but a dog will get used to anything really. The nice thing about a whistle is that you can call your dog, and no one knows that it's you, where as if you call 'Fido' really loudly then every will know that Fido's gone walkabout yet again.

If your dog isn't used to a whistle and you want to introduce it then just call his name and blow the whistle, when he comes give him a treat and send him away again, repeat a good few times until you think he's getting the hang of it, then start blowing the whistle first and call his name second. Again repeat a good few times, and then blow the whistle and pause, hopefully he'll start to come and see you getting the treat out so he'll keep coming. If he doesn't come, then whistle again and call his name afterwards. He will soon get the idea.

I use 'pip pip pip pip' as a come here signal, I use a long blast to mean 'sit down straight away and look at me for further instructions'.

You may be wondering why on earth I bother with being able to make him sit at a distance – it's actually sometimes very useful, if you are out in the country with no traffic about then a car appears on the horizon, it can be safer if your dog sits until the car has gone past. Or if you see something you weren't expecting, like a deer or a cat then again it can be handy to make him sit until what you don't want him to chase has gone, because don't forget he will sit and look at you for further instructions, so he may not spot the thing you don't want him to chase. Or even, and I admit this is just showing off here but why not, if you are in the park and another dog comes and plays with yours, but the stranger refuses to go back to his handler even when handler comes up to grab him, well if you can tell your dog to sit, it can allow the stranger to be grabbed by his handler, while allowing you to be very nonchalant and in control of the situation.

61. ADDITIONALLY

Enjoy your dog – it actually makes him behave better!

62. ANOTHER ADDITIONALLY

Remember, if you are teaching anything new, they learn best if it's one small step at a time, that way if the steps are easy then success is easy, and success breeds success

63. TWINS?

You might be thinking that puppies are a lot of trouble and take a lot of entertaining then it might be great fun to have two at the same time so that they can entertain each other, well yes, you've got a point and I'm willing to admit that some people do it and think it's a wonderful idea. But it has some down points which should be considered.

You've got to remember that you can never be as much fun to a puppy as their relationship with another puppy, and given the choice puppies will rather play with their litter mate than build up a relationship with you, this is just natural of course, don't take offence, but what you've got to do is to make the time to have a relationship with each puppy separately, you can't train two puppies at the same time, far better to have a puppy and have a relationship with it. The way I do things is to let the puppy grow into a middle aged dog and then get another puppy. That way the puppy, hopefully, gives a new lease of life to the middle aged one, but you are able to concentrate on the youngster, and it has the advantage that when your middle aged turns into a old dog and subsequently dies you still have one dog that can then 'baby sit' the new puppy that you are about to go out and buy. Remember if you buy two puppies at the same time you will hopefully end up eventually with two old dogs together, and if you've got a house and a way of life that will only fit two dogs then you might have to wait a long time for another puppy.

64. FEEDING TIME AGAIN.

I don't intend to tell you how to feed your dog; I just hope that you're aiming for a decent quality and a balanced diet. If by any chance you are using a dried food then can I just point out that it's not a good idea to tip the bag up and pour, it's very easy to overfeed, we all like to please our dogs and it's easy to give them a little bit extra. Use a measure of some sort, of the right size preferably so he can have a tin full at a time whichever member of the family is feeding the dog, and if he gets a little bit heavy then change if for a slightly smaller tin. A considerable number of dogs are too heavy which is a really terrible thing considering what it says about the owners, don't let it be yours. Remember if your dog is a puppy and still growing, and especially if he is a large/very large breed then being overweight may not be good for his joints and can have a bad result in the long run.

I don't offer this as a scientific cure only as an 'it happened to me'. I look after a labrador called Sam. Sam smelt bad, and I do mean bad, despite his owner bathing him regularly. Several years passed, and I persuaded his owner to change him onto a better quality food, in order to help his arthritis. About a month later his coat had gone soft and silky and he smelt 'normal' – it was wonderful; you could breathe without a gasmask!

65. I WISH HE'D STOP BARKING

Dogs bark, that's what they do, if you preferred something quieter then why didn't you get a cat? That said, there is a time when it's quite right for a dog to bark and a time they should really shut up. Little dogs seem to bark more than big ones, it seems to be a 'Napoleon' complex which you will see sometimes in little men. People do say that you will never get attacked by a barking dog, but some people said Hitler was a nice person.

I personally consider that my dogs are protecting my house if they bark when someone's at the door, they are alerting me to the danger – very risky person is my postman. That said, when I am aware, they should be quiet and let me deal with things, so if they bark, I say 'thank you - good girls' and that is the signal for them to now shut up, and if they keep barking then it's probable that I will say something like 'enough' in a tone of voice that implies I am no longer pleased and if they carry on I will be very unpleased. They know the situation.

If the dogs bark for no discernable reason then you have to either tell them to shut up, after all you probably have neighbours to consider, or if it's starting to be a habit, and they like the sound of their own voices, then you have to make them think that their bark causes something nasty to happen. What I'm suggesting is perhaps squirting them with water from a water pistol, perhaps rattling a plastic bottle filled with pebbles, basically you have to experiment with finding something that the dog doesn't like and then use that.

If the dog is out in the garden barking, then it's tempting to turn the telly up louder and ignore him, don't - that is not fair on your neighbours. Local kids can think it amusing to wind the dog up to bark, and it might well be tempting to start throwing things (such as bricks, mortar bombs, etc) at the kids. But that's really not the best idea, because they'll think it amusing to wind you up as well. You might have to resort to making sure your dog is in the house when the kids escape from school each day.

Don't tell the dog off; don't shout at the dog, or do anything that gives the game away that this is something that you don't like, the dog has to think that it is his bark that is causing this nasty thing to happen.

If your dog happens to join the local dog training class and then lets you down by barking at all the other dogs, you can either tell your dog you like this behaviour, well okay that translates into you ignoring him barking, or you can attempt to interrupt. One very good way of interrupting is by turning the dog away from the dog he is barking at, most dogs will very quickly decide they don't want to bark at somebody they can't see enough of to be sure he isn't going to sneak up behind them and attack.

If you've got the sort of dog that continuously barks at other dogs or people when he's out on a walk then you've got to think that it is possibly because the dog is anxious, if he's out the first time and he barks at someone that he doesn't like the look of <u>and then that person goes away,</u> then your dog has started to learn a behaviour that works for him. What you've got to do, and this may well involve you setting things up with a 'stooge' person, the stooge walks towards you, your dog barks, stooge comes closer towards you. Your dog goes quiet - stooge goes away. So all of a sudden the behaviour now doesn't work in his favour when he barks, but if he keeps quiet stooge goes away. Once your dog has started on behaviour that you like you can introduce things like rewards for keeping quiet when other dogs are about, so when your dog see's a dog or a person he doesn't like then not only is he not going to bark because that doesn't work, but handler is going to offer him a treat for focussing on handler when the strange dog comes close.

A word in sympathy with your barking dog here, some people and dogs deserve to be barked at, there are some strange people about! I wouldn't criticise some barking.

66. WHEN PINS AND NEEDLES MIGHT BE A GOOD THING

My first dog, Tacit, had a back problem of such severity that the prognosis was either an operation that they didn't know would work, or a life span of possibly six months. I didn't favour the operation, took her home and decided I would give spoil her for six months, dose her up on pain killers, and put her to sleep when she was suffering. In the meantime I decided to try acupuncture - she moved better, I happened to visit my parents and naturally told them about it, only to find that my father didn't believe in acupuncture - he said, and I can still remember his words 'they only believe in acupuncture because they think it will work', now I knew the dog was exceptionally clever but even I didn't believe she thought like that. Tacit got better and better and died of something totally unrelated about three years later. My second dog, Ticket, had a blood problem and had to go on steroids, unfortunately she went very lame and as she was on steroids the vet couldn't prescribe anything, I took her to the 'acupuncture lady', next day she was considerably better, the day after that she was 100 per cent sound. Now I don't believe in acupuncture, but luckily my dogs don't know that and they get better, so while I am sure it won't fix everything I know it's worth a try.

What I will add is that remember a conventional vet possibly makes more money from prescribing drugs to you and getting you to come back and see him, so he may not suggest acupuncture and he may rubbish the idea if you suggest it. Vets don't make money from healthy dogs.

There are other therapies that I have not tried and I can neither recommend them nor rubbish them. But I think you should consider them – if they tell you to do the opposite, drug wise, of what the conventional vets say then I'm not sure that I'm going to believe them, but if they aren't doing any harm then they might do some good.

67. EXCITEMENT IN YOUR LIFE

It might strike you as strange when your dog gets all excited because you're going out for a walk, but just think of how it would happen if he was a wild dog, this would mean that the pack was going hunting, and if they don't go hunting there is no way that wild dogs can go and open a tin of Doggy Chunks or shake out a packet of Doggy Bix - hunting means eating, it means surviving, possibly. No wonder it's exciting! So Fido is waiting fast asleep, but with one eye open because you usually go for a walk about now. And human puts their shoes on, excitement stirs, and human gets his coat out of the cupboard, we're up now and ready for action, and human takes the lead of the hook, we're standing at the door starting to jump up and down. And then human thinks I don't like this dog being this excited, so he sits down at the table and reads the paper – and the dog thinks 'oh b****r, I've got things wrong' and he settles down to go back to sleep again, and after a bit human seems to change his mind and gets up from the table to go out for a walk, and dog doesn't get as excited as he did first time, because he thinks Human might change his mind again, but this time human is happy about how less excited the dog is, and so he doesn't change his mind and they get to go out for a walk. It's all a question of expectations being fulfilled, the dog expects to go for a walk, if the expectation is not fulfilled then the next time he sees the right clues that means a walk he doesn't get so excited.

There's also another way that he's learning, he learns that if he stays calm he gets rewarded by going for a walk, and if he gets silly and objectionable then the human decides to do something else, unless your dog is very thick or very keen, and as long as you are prepared to be a bit devious and unpredictable, the lesson is usually learnt quickly.

68. 'EXPERTS'

I am not an expert on the subject of dogs, and I am certainly not an expert on your dog. I expect the sort of people who read this to be in an average situation with an average sort of dog. If you do have extreme problems then I suggest you venture further into more knowledgeable help than I can offer, and there's just one thing I want to point out here.

It is very popular at the moment for colleges to run courses for people to become 'experts' qualified to offer advice about dogs and charge people vast sums for such advice, these courses are naturally very trendy, a lot of people are tempted into the sort of lifestyle that it offers. Would I be cynical if I suggested that to get on these courses requires money, it certainly does not necessarily require you to actually own a dog, so this 'qualified' person that you are paying to advise you on your dog may not be sufficiently 'into' dogs to want to actually own and live with one, themselves. They might have the 'qualifications' they might talk very authoritatively, they might be charging a lot of money – they just might be talking b*******.

I am not an expert, I don't think I have met any experts - I have met a lot of people who know a lot about dogs, think about what I am saying - if anything sounds wrong to you think very carefully before going ahead.

69. I ADMIT I MIGHT BE PICKY

Now there are few things that I do admit I insist on, and yes, I admit they are because I am lazy. If I want to put a lead on my dog I insist it comes to me and lifts its head, why shouldn't it? It just makes life so much easier. If you watch people struggling with their dogs and running down the pavement to catch them then it makes sense. It's even more helpful when you take the lead off if the dog stands quietly; if the dog is pulling impatiently to get off the lead then it just makes the whole procedure so much more difficult. My dogs know the quickest way to get permission to run off is to stand there quietly, if it doesn't stand quietly it doesn't get to go off the lead. Furthermore, just because I've taken the lead off it doesn't mean that the dog is free to go running off, the dog gets its liberty when I tell it to go and play, sometimes I will tell the dog to walk to heel, and if it doesn't do this properly then it doesn't get its liberty. Permission to go and play is the best reward of all to most dogs, and if you are consistent then because it is such a high value reward this is one of the easiest things to teach any dog.

This has the added advantage for when you have your second dog. If first dog is already used to you taking the lead off and if he is used to standing there until you make up your mind, then this will let you take the lead of your second dog. If first dog disappears the instance you get the lead off, then second dog is not going to wait their quietly.

70. DOGS, FLOORS, CHAIRS, SOFAS, BEDS

The question is should you let your dog sit on the furniture? The answer is 'no definitely not if you are house proud' and, to my family's deep and everlasting disgust, I am not house proud. But not everything has totally gone to the dogs, this is still MY furniture not theirs, and they are only allowed to get on it when I give them permission, and that is not always granted, especially not when my mother's visiting. Some people never let their dogs on the furniture, and I am not saying that this is wrong, and some people let their dogs sit on whatever they want to, and I'm not saying that is wrong, but it's certainly a bit risky because it means that your furniture becomes their furniture and if you go down that route you risk losing your status as pack leader.

I was told by one individual that he allowed his dog to sit on the furniture, but it was okay because he exerted his authority by sometimes sitting in the dog's basket, the dog didn't mind – I don't think she noticed - she was asleep on the sofa!

71. UNFORTUNATELY YOU CAN'T AVOID . . .

Fleas happen. Usually heralded by a lot of scratching, and if you look closely your dog has a lot of little flecks of 'dirt' in his coat, it's actually flea pooh and it's mainly made up of your dog's blood that has been sucked up by the flea and digested and come out the other end. If you're 'lucky', (I put that in inverted commas, I don't think it's actually the right word to use) then you will be able to see one of the little b****** running around on the dogs coat, if you're really 'lucky' it will be running around on you. There are plenty of things available from the vets and shops to get rid of fleas. Unfortunately some of them are lethal to cats so be warned.

72. ANOTHER THING YOU PROBABLY CAN'T AVOID.

Another thing that you will probably get familiar with is ticks, whose life cycle is tied up with sheep and deer and things, they lurk on grasses and such like and when something such as your dog comes running by they climb aboard and then usually climb towards your dog's head, somewhere they will latch on and start sucking blood. They usually start the cycle about the size of an apple pip, when they get sucking blood they grow to the size of an inflated sweet corn kernel and then are sort of a grey mauve colour. You'll sometimes see them little, when they are black and you'll notice their eight little legs stuck out as they march along, or then you'll find them attached to your dog like a little lump – DON'T JUST PULL IT OFF. This is important, because if you try to remove it by brute force you will find that the body breaks off and leaves the head buried in your dog, and then it goes nasty and septic and proves painful to the dog. You can buy any number of tick removing gadgets, most of them little levers or tweezers like contraptions, you simply attach gently and rotate until the tick lets go and drops off. If you put the tick down on a surface you will often see it start to walk away, so if I say 'dispose of appropriately' you can use your imagination. It's not a bad idea if you wash the site and put on a bit of antiseptic, and you probably ought to wash your hands afterwards.

I should mention that some ticks carry Lyme disease, which is fairly serious if you or your dog gets it. Symptoms include fever, lameness, loss of appetite, sudden pain, arthritis, lethargy and a cough.

In all honesty I have only ever once had a tick attach itself to me, and it was dead when I found it.

73. WORMS

I'm not talking earthworms here, I'm talking about the sort of worms that your dog will have inside him. You need to think about worming your dog regularly, the vets recommend every three months. The half of the public that hate dogs say it's because dog faeces contain worms which cause their children to go blind, they might be unreasonable but why should they be frightened. There's two ways we can fight this rumour, by scooping the poop every time, and by worming dogs regularly.

74. FRESH AIR

You might have noticed all the adverts on the telly for air fresheners, particularly the plug-in sort; you might have them in your house already. I query whether they are sold for your benefit or the profit of the company that makes them; I also query whether they may be replaced by simply opening the windows occasionally. These plug-ins work by releasing chemicals into the air, they might want you to imagine that these chemicals are actually essences of fragrant meadows or bottled seaside but let's be realistic they're just chemicals that smell nice. If you can smell them then these chemicals are being breathed by your dog who, unlike you, doesn't go out to work for eight hours a day. I'm sure that all the companies will say their fresheners are perfectly safe, but people used to say the world was flat and cigarettes were good for you - if your dog has a cough or any sort of breathing difficulties it may be worth taking the air fresheners away for a couple of weeks and seeing what happens.

75. WALKIES

When you've got a new puppy and the sun is shining then everyone is keen to walk the dog, but when the novelty wears off and it's raining and everyone has been out at work all day and you probably just want to come home and slump in front of the telly. Please think of the dog, he's been shut in the house all day, yes it's briefly exciting when his owner comes home, and yes it's briefly exciting when he gets fed, but that's not enough. He needs to get out of the house for a walk. You chose him, not the other way round, you promised that you would feed and care for him for life, and educate and exercise him as well. I know walks would be better if he behaved better, but that means you have to educate him or be educated about what is going on, it's no good choosing not to walk him to avoid the problem arising because you will get a lot of other problems – if he is bored he will get fat, he will chew things, he might attack people and other dogs, he may bark incessantly and annoy the neighbours just for something to do, he will need to visit the vet more often because he will not be fit, you will get fat because you're not exercising, your clothes will shrink in the wash.

I could go on, I know the temptations, but you really can't ignore the needs of the dog – he needs exercise and mental stimulation on a daily basis!

76. BEWARE

Remember, dogs do not rely on a spoken language; they go in for reading 'body language' - for other dogs and also for you and all your family. So if you go up to your dog and your body is saying 'I expect my dog to run away' then your dog will probably oblige you and run away, alternatively it will probably bite you if you expect it to bite and jump up if you are expecting it to jump up, this is possibly why 'experts' can be so impressive – if they expect the dog to obey them then the dog will read the body language correctly and conclude this person is the pack leader and expects to be obeyed and think 'I'm not going to mess with him/her'. This gives you another problem if you are a submissive type of person; if you want your dog to recognise you as 'leader of the pack' then you have to act as if you believe you are 'leader of the pack' so it might be just an act initially but you have to walk tall, chest out, positive attitude and act as if you believe it will happen- soon it won't be just an act.

77. WHEN 'NORMAL' METHODS DON'T WORK

I had my first three dogs as puppies, and things went very well and I was of the opinion that my methods worked and would therefore work for every dog. Then I had a dog I renamed Sykes. The name Sykes is actually short for Psychopath! He was a year old working bred cocker spaniel and I knew that where he was currently living was not going to work and thought that either he was naturally a psychopath or with my innate talent and 'methods' he would settle down in a new place. A plus thing was that I already knew his litter brother and considered that he was an excellent 'normal' little dog. So Sykes came to live with me,

I mentioned it as a possibility to his current owners, the next day he was delivered and I should have been suspicious at the speed it was happening, he came in and peed up the furniture, then he dug holes in my lawn, chased leaves in my garden, and then spent many happy hours licking paving slabs wherever he could find them! He did have quite a few funny little habits.

Life was not initially happy, because Sykes seemed to 'lose the plot' whenever he got stressed, and as he got stressed whenever he was asked to do anything then he didn't learn much, and when he was stressed he wouldn't take a titbit or praise from you at all.

After several incidents of him running around loose amongst the traffic I was very disheartened and kept making lists of possible ways to re-home him including donating him to the foreign legion – I then bought a remote control collar. It's not an electric collar in that it doesn't administer an electric shock, it simply sprays a blast of water up under his chin, I tried it in the garden, I asked him to sit, he ignored me, I 'beeped' the collar, he ignored it, I asked him to sit again – he ignored it – I sprayed him, and he did not like that at all! But he didn't lose the plot like before, the next time I asked him to sit he ignored me, I beeped the collar and he thought about it and then he sat. The next day I took him for a walk up the woods, and he was fairly good, and then at the end we got to the car, the others got in, Sykes started to go for a run around which is what he did, and then I beeped the collar and he changed his mind and got in the car! And he was so not stressed that I was then able to praise him and give him many titbits.

At the moment, we're a month on, he wears the collar when he's out, he can go off the lead everywhere the other dogs can, I think the collar is for my benefit more than his, but I would not hesitate to recommend them for dogs that have already learnt that when they are off the lead they can ignore commands from the handler.

We're two months on from when I wrote the above, Sykes has learnt to ignore the spray collar when he wants to, but up to a point it has worked because it has given me the confidence to let him loose. He is improving slowly but he still had a long way to go. He is still very easily stressed when he's in the great outdoors so 'training' still has to progress extremely slowly. And I have to be careful not to allow him to indulge in silly excited behaviour.

Three months on, there's still a way to go but we're making slow progress. He's easier to stop going into manic behaviour at home, and as long as I read his behaviour I can anticipate difficult situations and avoid them. Out on walks up the wood he's very good and has slowed down from the rushing around behaviour that was his norm. If he's 'calm' I can make him walk to heel at the end and jump in the car to go home, and he will now stop on a walk and take a tit-bit from me.

And I did realise the other day, when I got him I thought he was an ugly little so and so, but I must admit that he's now relaxed and his face has lost the tension and he looks a lot better.

I took him for a session of the Ttouch method a week ago and that was interesting, it gave me the reassurance that I was going down the right route and gave me some methods to release the tension in him. I took all the dogs up the wood in the afternoon, we met some walkers who were slightly lost so I stopped to tell them which way to go, when I turned round Sykes was playing with their dog, and this was the first time he had ever been relaxed enough to play with a stranger.

A fortnight on and I've been poorly. Not desperately bad on deaths door sort of poorly, but more - okay I'll walk the dogs but things like the Tellington Ttouch method has got missed, this went on for five or six days, and then I realised that Sykes was going back to his ranting around the woods at ninety miles an hour and being deaf when he was called. I went back to his Tellington Ttouch method and he went back to being a steadier animal that has a chance of coming when he's called.

Okay we're six months on and Sykes is still living with me, and yes I would now be upset if he left - five months ago I would have given him away free with a packet of biscuits. With hindsight, and hindsight is a wonderful thing, I think all his problems stem from an inability to cope with stress. As a puppy if he had stress put on him he probably coped by rushing around, as he grew I think he went on to cope by rushing around, licking obsessively, and generally acting manically, and I think he chose not to interact with people and other dogs because it was less stressful.

I know that he didn't go to a 'proper' home until he was four months old, and I don't think that helped. When he did go to a home there were no other dogs living there, and I think that the fact that when he came to me and I already had two steady dogs he learned a lot from them. In his first home he had to cope with two children, one of which was very active - that definitely didn't help. His first owners were nice sensible people, but they were novice owners and I think that any novice owner would have been well out of their depth, they did not know to put a stop to his obsessive behaviour, it took me a while to work out that this was what I had to do, in fact when he came to live with me I just labelled him as 'special needs' Hopefully he will go on to improve further, I will always have to be careful that he doesn't get stressed and 'loose the plot' but I think there may be light at the end of the tunnel. I'm not pretending that he will ever be a little angel, in fact someone recently said that he seemed to be a 'normal' animal and that was the biggest compliment that I could have heard.

FURTHER READING

If you've got this far then I congratulate you, you might like to think about further reading. I would recommend 'Don't shoot the Dog' by Karen Pryor, a paperback that you will probably find in most good bookshops and you can certainly order over the internet. It won't tell you how to train your dog, there are plenty of good books that will tell you that, but it will tell you how to make your dog want to do what you want it to do. Think about the many Killer Whales that have been trained to do tricks in shows - you cannot influence a Killer Whale by giving it a good talking to whenever it does something wrong!, you have to use positive reward based methods. I think everyone ought to read this book because it will make you a better person, the principles apply to children, partners, work colleagues, dogs, chickens, virtually anything with a pulse – as well as killer whales of course.

WHERE DO WE GO FROM HERE?

Well I assume you're feeling either incredibly smug or incredibly lucky, no, let's assume you've been doing things right and that gives you permission to feel smug. But let me tell you one thing, you can bet your bottom dollar that your wonderful dog, who is perfectly capable of doing things excellently when no one is watching, well the first time you have a good audience all her training will go out of the window and she will let you down badly. That is just what dogs do; they are great for keeping egos in check.

You can just enjoy living in company with your dog, or you might like to think of doing some Agility training, not necessarily with a view to competing but just for fun, or perhaps there's flyball, or you might like to think about Gun dog work, or showing, just for fun possibly, after all you know that you've got the best dog anyway, or tracking, or anything really. Just enjoy!

WORDS THAT I USE

I'm only putting this in because I have been asked for it, it works for me and seems fairly logical – But I am definitely not saying they are the only words to use or that they are the best words to use.

COMMAND	SIGNAL	WHISTLE SIGNAL	MEANS
'Sit'	hand held at 45 degrees	Not appropriate	Put your bum on the floor Stay there until I tell you the next action
'Down'	held flat parallel to the floor	Not appropriate	Lie down now until I tell you something else
'Settle down'	hand held flat parallel to the floor	Not appropriate	Lie down, but get comfy because you're going to be there for a little time
'Fetch'	gesture showing hands empty and looking for something	Not appropriate	Go and get that which I threw or which I'm pointing at
'Find'	gesture showing hands empty and looking for something	Not appropriate	I know you don't know what you're looking for, and I don't know where it is so I can't send you in exactly the right direction, so go and look for something over there
'okay'	smile	Not appropriate	I've finished needing you to do what you've just been doing, now you can do what you want until I tell you otherwise
'Heel'	point to heel	Not appropriate	Don't go forward of my leg, this is free walking – if they are on the lead then they

			shouldn't be in front of my leg
'Here' or 'Here Fido'	stand with my arms outstretched and/or blow whistle	Quick peeps on the whistle, possibly three or four maximum	Get nearer to me -can be followed by
'Here'	pointing to the ground in front of me	Quick peeps on the whistle, possibly three or four maximum	I want you to come all the way to me
'Yes'	smile	Not appropriate	I know you don't really understand what you are meant to be doing, but what you are doing at this moment is actually right
'Wait'	could be a hand raised	Not appropriate	Just hold on a moment
'No'	looks stern	Not appropriate	If you do then I'm going to get cross
'Dead'	looks stern	Not appropriate	Release whatever you've got in your mouth into my hands
'Sit'	hand and arm raised at 45 degrees	Long toot on the whistle	Sit wherever you are and whatever you're doing and look at me

If you've read this book to the end then please can I ask you a favour?

Do not give the book away to a friend or a relation, by all means buy them a copy for Christmas or tell them to go and buy their own copy.

Instead put this book on the shelf and in six months time please make an effort to look at it again, so that you will be reminded of all those good resolutions that you made six months ago and have since let slip.

A good relationship with your dog is something to be worked on and treasured and nurtured – and the work that you put into the relationship will be rewarded.

Printed in the United Kingdom by
Lightning Source UK Ltd., Milton Keynes
139736UK00001B/51/P